REMINISCENCES
OF MY LIFE IN CAMP

Susie King Taylor.

REMINISCENCES
OF MY LIFE IN CAMP

*An African American Woman's
Civil War Memoir*

SUSIE KING TAYLOR

Introduction by Catherine Clinton

THE UNIVERSITY OF GEORGIA PRESS
Athens & London

Frontispiece: Portrait and signature of Susie King Taylor.
From the original 1902 edition.

Paperback edition published in 2006 by
The University of Georgia Press
Athens, Georgia 30602
www.ugapress.org
Introduction © 2006 by The University of Georgia Press
All rights reserved

Printed digitally

Library of Congress Cataloging-in-Publication Data
Taylor, Susie King, b. 1848.
Reminiscences of my life in camp : an African American woman's
Civil War memoir / Susie King Taylor; introduction by
Catherine Clinton.
xl, 76 p. : ill., ports. ; 18 cm.
ISBN-13: 978-0-8203-2666-5 (paperback : alk. paper)
ISBN-10: 0-8203-2666-6 (paperback : alk. paper)
1. Taylor, Susie King, b. 1848. 2. United States. Army. Colored
Infantry Regiment, 33rd (1864–1866) 3. United States —
History — Civil War, 1861–1865 — Regimental histories. 4. United
States — History — Civil War, 1861–1865 — Personal narratives.
5. United States — History — Civil War, 1861–1865 —
African Americans. 6. United States — History — Civil War,
1861–1865 — Women. 7. African American women — Biography.
8. Freedmen — United States — Biography. 9. Nurses — United
States — Biography. I. Title.
E492.94 33rd .T3 2006
973.7'75'092 — dc22 [B]
2005018811

British Library Cataloging-in-Publication Data available

CONTENTS

APPENDIX

INTRODUCTION

LET US NOT FORGET THAT TERRIBLE WAR
Catherine Clinton

Susie King Taylor was born into bondage on August 6, 1848, on a Georgia plantation during the high tide of southern slavery. A respected clubwoman and author, she settled among the ebony Brahmins, as the black elite of Boston were known. She prepared her life story for publication in 1902 as a kind of tribute to the cause of the Union soldiers with whom she served during the American Civil War. Many such regimental histories and wartime memoirs appeared at the turn of the century, but Taylor's volume, being written by a woman, was rare. Susie King Taylor died in 1912.

Taylor's reminiscences appeared at a time when military memoirs of the Civil War were particularly in vogue, especially following the Spanish American War—when soldiers from the previously Confederate states fought side by side with their former enemies, a healing process much-celebrated in the late 1890s.[1] Both Yankee and Confederate veterans had begun to capitalize on the interest in Civil War exploits, and partisan publications blossomed in the mid-1870s, exemplified by George Cary Eggleston's *A Rebel's Rec-*

ollections (1874) and William Tecumseh Sherman's two-volume *Memoirs* (1875). As David Blight has demonstrated in *Race and Reunion: The Civil War in American Memory*, an entire cottage industry grew in response to the insatiable appetite for Civil War lore (a hunger that seems surprisingly vibrant well into the twenty-first century!).[2]

In the decades following the surrender at Appomattox, northerners maintained a steady interest in military history of the war, especially following the publication of *The War of the Rebellion: A Compilation of the Official Records of the Union and Confederate Armies* (beginning in the 1880s) and the appearance of what was to become a classic of the genre, *The Personal Memoirs of U. S. Grant* (1885–86). At the same time, white southerners churned out nostalgic chronicles of the era "before the war," plantation epics that seized on the popular imagination.[3] Some Yankees fought back with their own counterchronicles, many in the form of memoirs of their days with the Underground Railroad.[4] Susie King Taylor's recollections appeared at a time when dueling interpretations of bygone days continued to fascinate.

Her volume featured an introduction by Thomas Wentworth Higginson, the Boston aristocrat who commanded black Union soldiers in South Carolina, where Susie King served as a teacher, a laundress, and a nurse. Higginson had published his own memoir, *Army Life in a Black Regiment* (1870).[5] As a former comrade from their days in the South Carolina campaign, she sent him her own manuscript for his assistance. Higginson confessed to only a light editorial hand, correcting a few proper names. When the book was published in Boston in 1902, Taylor dedicated it to her patron.

The record of her shift from slavery to freedom is a poignant tale and contributes to the slave narrative. Ex-slaves wrote well over one hundred book-length narratives during the slaveholding era.[6] This does not include the scores of memoirs written by blacks in the period following emancipation. Nor does it include the oral and written testimony collected by Federal Writers' Project of the Works Progress Administration during the 1930s—a collection known as the WPA narratives.[7]

Of the published slave narratives, less than 10 percent were written by women, and only one, Harriet Jacobs's *Incidents in the Life of a Slave Girl Written by Herself*, has gained any following, as opposed to the half-dozen male narratives that have received widespread critical and popular attention, most notably those of Frederick Douglass. Similarly, men penned almost all the eyewitness testimony about the black experience during the Civil War.[8] Charlotte Forten's chronicle of her experience in the Sea Islands, which first appeared in the pages of the *Atlantic Monthly*, is an extraordinary but rare example of female perspective.[9] Women composed even fewer of the post–Civil War memoirs: Elizabeth Keckly's *Behind the Scenes* is perhaps the best known and the most exceptional.[10] Many fewer black women's autobiographies in the nineteenth century feature wartime experiences.[11] Thus Taylor's book is distinctive and singular because it remains the only published account by a black woman serving with the military during the Civil War. Thanks to the important scholarly work of the past quarter century, we now have a much better understanding of women's experiences during the Civil War.[12] Even so, first-person testimony by African American women was rarely preserved, which makes Taylor's work all the more invaluable. Her memoir showcases Taylor's experiences as a nurse and teacher, a laundress and an organizer, and it reminds readers of the unheralded Civil War contributions by women. Women volunteers, women nurses, and women's sacrifices in this important domain have only recently elicited scholarly attention.[13]

Taylor's volume offers insight into the layered meanings of the freedom experience for African Americans — how someone like Susie King Taylor was so very pleased and seemingly surprised to be given cordial treatment by "white ladies" such as the quartermaster's wife and Clara Barton.[14] The war as a catalyst for African American freedom, as witnessed in first-person African American chronicles, remains a significant but relatively rare historical source. New works are often unearthed, but the number of accounts remains relatively small.[15]

Susie King Taylor composed her memoir in the wake of a return visit to former Confederate states — states considerably blighted by Jim Crow segregation. She experienced separate and unequal conditions for blacks and saw the lack of political and economic opportunities for her brethren — in sum, she witnessed a return to white supremacy. Human rights were endangered, as the southern landscape was dotted with the bodies of lynched blacks. The turn of the twentieth century was a time of engulfing dread for African Americans.[16]

Taylor had been a part of a rising tide of self-emancipated slaves engaged in the battle for liberation. She was one of the hundreds upon thousands who fled to federal lines and fought for the restoration of the Union and an end to slavery. As a young girl of thirteen, she had risked all for freedom in 1862—running away from Liberty County, Georgia, to join the ranks of the "contrabands," slaves who escaped from Confederate masters. What set this remarkable woman's career in motion? And what led her to pen this scolding memoir at age fifty-four?

Unfortunately, we have little but Taylor's published recollections to help us puzzle her motives. In fact, we have few historical facts about her beyond those included in her memoir. A photograph of Taylor in her nurse's uniform adorns the front pages of her book—a black woman appearing both feminine and patriotic, stalwart yet demure.

This image provided a direct counterpoint to popular stereotypes of African American women, caricatures that portrayed women of color as hypersexual and bestial—or contrarily as obsequious mammies.[17] Beyond her dignified photographic image, Taylor presented a powerful portrait of herself within the pages of her *Reminiscences.* The accounts of her life in camp, as well as her experiences before and after, provide compelling insights into black womanhood during this dramatic era of social change.

The esteem Taylor gained by participating in the liberation of her people was part of a family tradition, which included black forefathers who fought against the British during the American Revolution. Born in Liberty County, Georgia, Susie was the first child of Hagar, an enslaved woman, and Raymond Baker. Her mother's mother, Dolly Reed, played a formative role in Susie's upbringing. From the age of seven, she was raised in her grandmother's Savannah home.

Many slaves had no record of genealogies for their families, especially during the booming era of territorial expansion following the American Revolution. As hundreds of thousands of enslaved persons were transported to the frontier, Africans and their descendants endured a migration equal to or greater than that of the transatlantic diaspora.[18] From a very young age, children were commonly sold to populate the borderlands. As a result many complained, as did black abolitionist Samuel R. Ward, "Like the sources of the Nile, my ancestry, I am free to admit, is rather difficult of tracing."[19]

Susie King Taylor may not have had the exact dates and names of her ancestors, but she was descended from a long line of proud females who passed on their stories to their daughters and instilled in them a sense of pride in heritage that was not dimmed by generations of bondage.[20]

Dolly Reed, Susie Baker's grandmother, instilled in her at a very young age the pride of family. After her son James died at the age of twelve, Dolly had poured her devotion into her only remaining child, Hagar, and Hagar's three children who came to live with her. Although Susie's grandmother lived in Savannah, she was a frequent visitor to Susie's Liberty County birthplace, nearly forty miles away. Whether Dolly Reed was an emancipated or a hired-out slave is unknown, but her movements were still supervised by her sponsor and (perhaps former) owner, Valentine Grest, whose signature was necessary for Reed—as a black woman—to maintain residence in Savannah.[21] Grest also owned Dolly Reed's only living child and her grandchildren. In 1856, when Susie was only seven years old, Dolly Reed persuaded the Grests to send Susie to live in Savannah. It was a rare privilege to reside with a grandmother in the city rather than be sent into the fields or sold away—both common fates for enslaved children in Georgia.[22]

Savannah offered the opportunity for a precious commodity denied to most blacks in the South: education. At a time when only 5 percent of Georgia blacks were literate, when a plantation slave caught writing might have his or her thumb cut off as punishment, the former state capital, Savannah, was a Mecca for black learning.[23] Reed was able to send her grandchildren to a "bucket school" run by a free black woman, Mary Woodhouse.

Woodhouse took in anywhere from twenty-five to thirty black children, who secretly made their way to their schoolroom, staggering arrivals and hiding texts in "buckets" or wrapped in newspapers.[24] After Susie became proficient at the alphabet, she was promoted to a school run by Mary Beasley.

Stealth and disguise were essential at a time when teaching slave children was a crime. Savannah educator James M. Simms, a free black, did not turn away enslaved pupils, teaching them side by side with his free black students, a practice that provoked the wrath of white authorities. They closed his school and put Simms under arrest, then fined and publicly whipped him for his "crime."[25] Shortly thereafter, Simms sailed for Boston.[26]

Despite setbacks, blacks in Savannah enjoyed advantages denied to their rural brothers and sisters, privileges afforded to Susie Baker while living with her grandmother. She was allowed to attend the Christ Episcopal Church, where a handful of black communicants, including Mary Woodhouse, worshipped.[27] Of the 185 pupils in the Christ Episcopal Sunday School in 1854, 100 were black.[28]

By 1860 when she was eleven, Susie Baker had outgrown the underground schools for African American children. She begged her childhood playmate and white neighbor, Katie O'Connor, to share her books and lessons. O'Connor's mother agreed, but after only a few months, O'Connor entered a convent. When Susie pleaded with her grandmother to locate another teacher, Reed hired her landlord's son, James Blouis, who was willing to offer the twelve-year-old lessons. He kept his tutoring totally secret, and Susie's lessons continued until the Civil War intervened. As members of the Savannah Volunteer Guards, James and his brother Eugene were drafted to fight in the war following the firing on Fort Sumter in April 1861. Thus ended Susie Baker's formal lessons.

When war finally erupted, blacks in Savannah, free and enslaved, engaged in an even more dangerous underground — holding political meetings in deserted buildings and churches, breaking curfew (as blacks were not allowed on the streets at night without passes).[29] Susie Baker was drawn into this political intrigue, because literacy allowed her to forge passes for those needing to travel the streets at night. Though only thirteen at the time, Baker was in the thick of black resistance and racial intrigue.

During a raid on a church, Dolly Reed was arrested for breaking curfew and singing hymns that authorities branded as treasonous — gospels with lines such as "we shall all be free." Susie, valuable slave property, returned to the Grest estate in Liberty County, arriving on April 1, 1862.

A long siege resulted in the fall of Fort Pulaski, on April 11, 1862 — an important objective for Union military commanders seeking a strategic point of entry for operations along the northern Georgia coast. Susie decided to seize an opportunity for freedom and took off with her uncle and cousins in search of federal protection behind Union lines.

With the Union's capture of Port Royal on the South Carolina coast on November 7, 1861, the North had gained a foothold within the Confederacy, one that would particularly please the Union. South Carolina had been the first state to secede, and capture of the port was key to the North's strategy to infiltrate and cripple the Confederacy's hold on the surrounding area.

The seacoast of South Carolina and Georgia boasted some of the most fertile land in the region, where the finest cotton, known as "Sea Island cotton," was grown. Once Union soldiers entered the territory, they found scores of abandoned plantations and hundreds of abandoned slaves. The addition of fugitive slaves from inland fleeing to the new Union camps along the coastline became a major problem for the federal army. Susie and her relatives ended up among these fugitives on St. Catherines Island, one of the northernmost of Georgia's Golden Isles.[30]

The Yankees put the fugitives to work. Northern papers reported in December 1861 that "the cotton upon these islands is being picked by the contrabands, under the direction of our officers. About two million dollars worth of cotton has already been secured."[31] By March 1862 the Union had conquered sufficient territory for Secretary of War Edwin Stanton to designate Georgia, Florida, and South Carolina as the Department of the South, a key milestone in the Union campaign to subdue and recapture rebel territory. Major General David Hunter was appointed commander in charge of the region.

The U.S. Treasury Department, in combination with private enterprise — the New England Freedmen's Aid Society, the National Freedmen's Relief Association of New York, and the Pennsylvania Freedmen's Relief Association — organized an important relief campaign to educate, train, and assist former slaves to become self-supporting.[32] Christened the "Port Royal Experiment," the campaign was intended to allow New England reformers to demonstrate that freed people would become industrious when given half a chance. Many young idealists heeded the call to become part of the "Gideon's Band," the volunteer organization of teachers who would carry out the experiment.[33]

Other kinds of experiments and battles progressed throughout the region, as South Carolina became one of the flashpoints where the debate over recruiting blacks into the military was most hotly contested. Charleston was, of course, the Cradle of Secession, where armed conflict commenced with the standoff at Fort Sumter in April 1861. The haughtiness and intractability of this Confederate stronghold raised the stakes for invading Union military, just as the hundreds and then thousands of "disloyal" slaves who fled Rebel masters for Union lines became an undermining threat.

From the war's earliest days, African Americans had demanded to take their place in the front ranks of combat. Independent black units, such as the Hannibal Guards in Pittsburgh, rallied round the cause but were not welcome in the Union ranks because of color prejudice. Complaining that the Union could not fight with one hand behind its back, Frederick Douglass and other African American leaders advocated black enlistment. Douglass saw military service as an important step along the road to black equality: "Once let the black man get upon his person the brass letters U.S.; let him get an eagle on his button, and a musket on his shoulder, and bullets in his pocket, and there is no power on the earth which can deny that he has earned the right of citizenship in the United States."[34]

Abraham Lincoln had been reluctant to allow African Americans to serve in the military and wished to appease the border states still loyal to the Union, such as Maryland and Delaware, where slavery remained in force. Washington brass began to warm to the idea of stealing away Rebels' slaves, even if they resisted the idea of slaves as soldiers. Major General David Hunter not only insisted that the army employ ex-slaves as laborers but also demanded, as Frederick Douglass advocated, that they be allowed to prove themselves in combat.[35]

Hunter detested planters who came into Union camps complaining about runaway slaves. Some Union officers turned fugitives back over to owners willing to beg for them. Hunter insisted that the military put a stop to this practice. He was not alone among the Union command to hold such strong abolitionist views. Many Yankee politicians and black activists opposed Lincoln's appeasement policy. They wanted an unambiguous condemnation of slaveholding, to bring things to a head. These radicals hoped to shift the goals for Union triumph from a purely military realm to include moral considerations.

On May 9, 1862, after less than two months on the job as head of the Department of the South, Hunter took matters into his own hands and declared "the persons in these three States, Georgia, Florida, and South Carolina, heretofore held as slaves, are therefore declared forever free."[36] Hunter directed officers to begin rounding up able-bodied African Americans for federal army use. He was passionate about his dream of "negro regiments" and determined to move ahead, even if the government dragged its feet.

Whatever his personal feelings about slavery at the time—and many believe by this point he was tilting toward emancipation—Lincoln did not want military men dictating policy. On May 19, Lincoln voided the Department of the South's emancipation edict. Hunter licked his wounds and, bowing to pressure, disbanded the black South Carolina regiment he had organized from fugitive slaves in the region. He insisted that since he was never officially "censured," he was just a victim of bad timing.

Doubtless Hunter felt vindicated when Congress passed the Second Confiscation Act in July 1862, which freed all slaves whose masters were Rebels, and a Militia Act that allowed these "forever . . . free" blacks to be enlisted by the military as paid laborers.

This dream of black soldiers looked to become a reality in the wake of Lincoln's preliminary Emancipation Proclamation in September 1862. Brigadier General Rufus Saxton, appointed to supervise contraband affairs, organized former slaves into regiments, regiments such as those headed by Thomas Wentworth Higginson, who was recruited to South Carolina for this noble effort. Higginson was a Harvard trained minister who became deeply involved in radical abolitionism in the 1850s. A sympathizer to the cause of John Brown, Higginson was eager to take on the role of officer in a black regiment when he sailed down from Massachusetts to Port Royal to assume his commission in the fall of 1862.

Many blacks in the region had been waiting for this signal and a chance to don a uniform to join the fight. Such was the heady atmosphere when Susie Baker headed for freedom in 1862.

Within a fortnight of Susie's arrival behind federal lines, Union commanders transported her with a large contingent of fugitives by boat to St. Simons Island, a federal stronghold farther south along the coast. When the officer in charge of the evacuation found that Susie was literate, articulate, and mature beyond her years, she was invited to run a school for contrabands on the island. She consented and obtained a promise of books, which arrived from the North within a matter of weeks. She was assigned forty young children by day, and a number of adults attended night classes. The makeshift school lasted until the late fall of 1862, when Susie and other refugees were relocated to Beaufort, South Carolina.

Susie Baker arrived in the Sea Islands when the former First South Carolina Volunteers were preparing to officially join the Union army as part of the reconstituted Company E, the Thirty-third Regiment of the United States Colored Troops (USCT). She devoted herself to the men of the Thirty-third. Her uncles and cousins joined, as did Edward King, a young carpenter from Georgia whom Susie had known before the war. King had escaped his master to volunteer for the Union. King and Baker became close and eventually married. Although the exact date is unknown, they were wed late in 1862 or in the earliest weeks of 1863.

This was a historic moment of great promise and hope for liberated blacks in the South. On January 1, 1863, the Emancipation Proclamation ushered in not just a new year but a whole new era. In Washington, the Reverend Henry McNeal Turner, an AME pastor, read a copy of Lincoln's proclamation to a cheering crowd gathered at the White House, where the jubilant response was nearly deafening.[37]

Official ceremonies organized by General Saxton for soldiers and civilians in occupied South Carolina were both elaborate and poignant. Anticipating a crowd of several thousand, the Union commander ordered the roasting of twelve oxen for a celebratory feast. Crowds were ferried in by boat to the former Smith plantation where the First South Carolina tented at Camp Saxton. Soldiers at the wharf escorted guests to the middle of a large grove where a platform had been set up for speakers. A regimental band played and spirits were high when festivities commenced shortly before noon. This three-hour program of prayer, hymns, and speeches washed over the assembled crowd.

Following the presentation of the regimental flag, a quavering voice from the audience unexpectedly broke into song—"My country 'tis of Thee"—and soon the entire crowd joined in for several verses. When the singing ended, Colonel Higginson, flag in hand, was so moved that he confessed it was difficult for him to find his voice; but after collecting himself, he offered a stirring speech. The formal program resumed and soldiers joined in singing "John Brown's Body" and other favorite songs. For those gathered near Port Royal, it was a turning point on the road to freedom that few would forget.[38]

For Susie Baker King, it was the dawn of a new era as well. As a freed black woman, the fourteen-year-old bride took on enormous responsibilities when the contraband pupils she had been teaching were transformed into Union soldiers. She became devoted to these men and aided her husband's regiment. She officially served the military in her capacity as a laundress—but confessed "I did very little of it, because I was always busy doing other things" (35). The health of the men was a primary focus, as three out of five soldiers who died during the war succumbed to disease unrelated to combat.[39] Although less than 2 percent of black soldiers were killed in combat (compared to 6 percent of white soldiers), death from disease was a deadly 20 percent for black troops—double the death rate from disease for white troops.[40]

Black troops suffered distinct disadvantage from the lack of proper medical attention. White doctors rarely served black units, although fifty-eight black regiments were in the field by October 1863. Medical care fell on the shoulders of nurses, who tried to alleviate the sufferings of the soldiers.[41] Camp life presented an extraordinary challenge, especially in the South, to trying to keep troops healthy. Newlywed King committed herself to the well-being of "our boys," as she called them, although she was younger than most of the members of the regiment.

Union surgeons found King a skilled assistant, as she switched from washing bandages to applying them, moving into nursing duties. Her rapid acclimation was a necessity. "We are able to see the most sickening sights," she wrote, "such as men with their limbs blown off and mangled by the deadly shell, without a shudder; and instead of turning away, how we hurry to assist in alleviating their pain, bind up their wounds, and press the cool water to their parched lips" (31–32).

Clara Barton launched an independent medical crusade during the Civil War and would later found the American Red Cross.[42] She arrived in Beaufort in the spring of 1863 and was appalled by the primitive conditions suffered by the wounded. She set about establishing her own independent brand of discipline. After she dined with Colonel Higginson in June, she toured General Hospital Number Ten, where she met Susie King and visited the men in the wards.[43] King enjoyed the older woman's camaraderie: "Miss Barton was always very cordial toward me, and I honored her for her devotion and care of those men" (30).

Susie King stood ready when Union troops were battered and repelled on the parapets of Fort Wagner during their famous assault in July 1863.[44] This crucial fort was located on the northern tip of Morris Island, a few miles south of Charleston. The Union command believed this bastion held the key to the harbor. If the Yankees could take control, they might cripple blockade running along the coast and pave the way for conquest of Charleston.

The Union command faced extraordinary obstacles

in plotting their assault, as the fort was practically im-
pregnable. Waves washed up to the eastern wall at high
tide, and marshes and bogs covered the ground leading to the other three walls. Further, the Rebels ringed
the fort's walls with a moat as well as a rifle pit. With
over seventeen artillery guns aimed outward, the fort
seemed invincible — but a prize Yankees eagerly sought.
On July 18, the Union command launched their attack,
with Colonel Robert Gould Shaw's Massachusetts
Fifty-fourth leading the charge.[45]

After hours of bloody battle, lasting well past midnight, the Union assault failed — although federal
units, especially African American soldiers, had fought
bravely and well. By the wee hours of July 19, many
Union soldiers lay injured on the beach; when the tide
came in, many drowned before being rescued by litter
bearers coming to collect the wounded.

When July 19 dawned, an eyewitness reported the
gruesome scene:

> blood, mud, water, brains and human hair melted to-
> gether; men lying in every possible attitude ... their
> limbs bent into unnatural shapes by the fall of twenty
> or more feet; the fingers rigid and outstretched, as if
> they had clutched at the earth to save themselves.[46]

Of the five thousand Union men engaged at Fort
Wagner, more than 1,500 men (including 111 officers)
were killed, wounded, or captured.[47] Susie King cared
for survivors brought into the hospital tents and faith-
fully attended her troops.

Camp life was fraught with peril. Taylor reported

that she "learned to handle a musket very well. . . . I assisted in cleaning the guns and used to fire them off, to see if the cartridges were dry, before cleaning and reloading, each day" (26). In addition, she told of night-time disruptions—hearing gunfire, being forced to dress quickly, preparing to flee, as "night was the time the rebels would try to get into our lines" (50–51).

But life in camp was staid compared to what soldiers faced during their forays. While moving from Augusta, Georgia, to Hamburg, South Carolina, some of the black soldiers ran into "bushwhackers," Rebels lying in wait. Many would sneak up on sleeping black soldiers and cut their throats. When a Confederate was caught in the act of attempted murder, King reported, his trial and subsequent execution were meant to put a stop to these deadly assassinations (43–44).

On February 28, 1865, the men of the Thirty-third marched victoriously into Charleston. The soldiers helped put out the fires left behind by evacuating Confederates. Within a few weeks, the war was over and Susie Baker King and her husband returned to Savannah.

Taylor's memoir chronicles the exploits of valiant black men in blue, as any regimental history might. But her book is much more; the volume is at least partially intended as a rebuke of the age of amnesia in which Taylor wrote. This not-so-gentle scolding was aimed at several audiences.

Disheartened that the sacrifice of United States Colored Troops has not been given wider recognition, she suggests that readers need to "appreciate the old soldiers" (51). She recalls the high hopes shared when the regiment was mustered out. Their beloved leader, Lieutenant Colonel Charles T. Trowbridge, had expressed his belief that Fort Wagner would become a shrine "where in the future your children's children will come on pilgrimages to do homage to the ashes of those who fell in this glorious struggle" (48). These hopes and dreams might have disappeared in the ensuing years, but Susie King Taylor held onto a copy of Trowbridge's speech, vowing to keep it with her for the rest of her days.

Although the assault on Fort Wagner was celebrated at the time in the press and later with ceremonies and memorials, Colonel Robert Gould Shaw, the fallen white commander from Boston, garnered the lion's share of glory. Shaw's heroism was burnished in bronze with the dedication of Augustus Saint-Gaudens's gilded statue on the Boston Common in 1897.[48] William Carney, the heroic black sergeant from New Bedford who suffered four wounds saving the regimental colors from the parapets of the Confederate fort, was present at the dedication of the Shaw memorial. The only African American on the platform, he received a standing ovation. Yet Carney had not yet received the Congressional Medal of Honor for which he had been nominated. The medal was finally awarded in 1900, when Carney became the first African American to earn this coveted military honor.[49]

Not until the renaissance of African American studies in the 1970s was the role of the black soldier in the

Civil War more widely appreciated. Edward Zwick's 1989 film, *Glory*, generated even more popular interest in this historical event. In 1996 a memorial to the black soldiers of the Civil War was finally erected in Washington, D.C.

Nearly a century earlier, Susie King was right to be disheartened. African Americans across the South were fighting the roadblocks that whites in former Confederate states mounted to prevent ex-slaves from assuming their roles as citizens. In the wake of surrender, many former Confederates tried to wrest control of newly assembled state legislatures and push through repressive legislation that became known collectively as "Black Codes," laws seeking to enforce racial inequality. White legislators, for example, attempted to restrict the mobility of black citizens through vagrancy laws, to favor white employers over black employees, and to throw former slaves into jail—and into the arms of a repressive convict lease system—on the flimsiest of evidence. These Black Codes were struck down, but they represented the fierceness of resistance that white southerners raised to block African Americans' pursuit of civil rights.[50]

Because knowledge and literacy were viewed as keystones for permanent freedom, education became a primary focus for African American reformers of the post–Civil War era.[51] After the war, Susie King returned to Savannah and set up an academy in her home, charging each of her twenty pupils only a dollar a month and offering lessons to adults in the evenings. Schools were a priority for freed people, although the struggle for economic survival was paramount during this tumultuous time.

As early as January 1865, black clergy founded the Savannah Education Association, funding the operation with an eight-hundred-dollar donation. Louis B. Toomer was the principal teacher, supervising fifteen instructors. When the American Missionary Association (AMA) arrived on the scene in coastal Georgia and discovered this enterprising African American educational operation, they were stunned. The AMA wanted to supervise these independent schools, but blacks resisted mightily.[52]

Tragedy struck when Edward King was killed in an accident at the docks in September 1866, and Susie was left behind a pregnant widow. After her son was born in 1867, King tried to run a school in Liberty County, Georgia, but after a year, she returned to Savannah to live with her widowed mother, who ran a dry goods store. Susie King's father, Raymond Baker, had served on a Union gunboat during the war and had died in 1867 (64–65). In 1868, Susie King took another stab at teaching in Savannah, offering evening classes for adults—but the American Missionary Association's free enterprise, the Beach Institute, forced her to close shop.[53] The two black women, mother and daughter, struggled to survive and care for Susie's son.

Many ex-slaves found it difficult to stem the tide of southern white prejudice and northern indifference during Reconstruction, the era of federal rule following victory at Appomattox. African Americans in the South were severely disappointed by the outcome of the election of 1876 and settled with a "corrupt bargain." The Democratic candidate, Samuel Tilden, conceded the election to Republican Rutherford B. Hayes, and in return, federal troops were withdrawn from the South. This compromise signaled a severe setback for African American civil and political rights. Blacks found their hard-won gains slipping away as white southerners reinstituted second-class citizenship with Jim Crow legislation.

This period marked the emergence of protest movements for domestic migration within the United States, such as those led by "Pap" Singleton and other Exodusters.[54] Liberia, a country in western Africa founded by ex–American slaves, became the focus of international emigrationist movements, spearheaded by Martin Delany and other radical black leaders.[55]

Impoverished and devoid of alternatives, Susie King joined the growing ranks of black women in the post–Civil War era forced into domestic service. By 1868 she had to leave her son with her widowed mother while she "lived in" as a household servant. She was offered positions with a series of southern employers, one of whom took her on family holidays to the North during summers. She found this exposure both eye opening and thrilling. Racism was present both in the North and the South, but within the postbellum North, African Americans carved out autonomous communities, where black women operated schools and clubs, participated in religious and civic activities, and contributed to an atmosphere of racial reform. By her sojourns out of the South, Susie King was exposed to a much more thriving, diverse climate of opportunity for women of color.

King eventually relocated to Massachusetts in 1874 and held a series of positions as a domestic servant until she wed Bostonian Russell Taylor in 1879. Following her remarriage, the thirty-one-year-old Susie King Taylor retired from domestic service to keep her own house. She became a respected clubwoman and in 1886 organized a woman's auxiliary of the Grand Army of the Republic (GAR), the Union veterans' group. The GAR sponsored reunions and civic campaigns, reaching out to all former soldiers. She served in several capacities within the auxiliary, finally assuming the role of group president in 1893.

In 1896, as part of a GAR project, Taylor compiled a list of war veterans living in Massachusetts. This veterans' census enabled her to link up with old comrades. Even more, the project embodied an "official record," one she undertook with pride. Her list of the Thirty-third Regiment served as an appendix for her published reminiscences.

In 1898 Taylor received a dire plea from her son, an actor with a traveling theater company, who lay desperately ill in Shreveport, Louisiana. Her journey to help him and the obstacles she faced form a dramatic ending to her reminiscences. She had returned to the former Confederacy at least once since her remarriage, a pilgrimage to Savannah to see her dying grandmother in 1888 (3–4). Yet when she received her son's summons, she had not been back to Dixie in over a decade.

In 1896 the Supreme Court ruling *Plessy v. Ferguson*

had declared "separate but equal" the law of the land. Southern lawmakers, however, were not afraid of accountability, and they enforced white supremacy with no fears of repercussions. Thus Taylor's southern journey in 1898 was jarring and far from sentimental. Denied access to accommodations that were for whites only on her train ride south, Taylor was forced to sit in a smoking car (69). She was in Shreveport when a black porter was murdered in cold blood for his "saucy" answer to a white man, and the white man got off scot-free (72–73).

Racism's horrors hit home even more when she was unable to secure proper medical care for her son. She could not purchase a ticket for a sleeping car to take him north for effective medical treatment. She nursed him alone and then, following his death, was forced to bury him in Shreveport. On her sad trip home, she witnessed a lynching in Clarksdale, Mississippi (74). Taylor raged that the South preached "civilization" while promoting barbarity, as blacks suffered indignities, deprivations, and worse.

Rather than sinking into bitter despair, Taylor imagined a time when justice for African Americans would arrive in the South. She declared with forbearance that not all whites should be blamed for the "few of the race" guilty of hatred and racism. She employed biblical language, comparing her race with the children of Israel and invoking images of Christian redemption. Her memoir contains poetry and power, as she asserts that progress "will come in time, surely if slowly" (75).

Despite these hopeful suggestions, a pervasive air of

melancholy hangs over her conclusion. Taylor escaped southern racism and made a new life for herself in the North. Yet she felt an ache of sorrow about the losses that she and her nation had endured. She maintained a bond with many surviving members of her regiment but resented the fact that by century's end she could ask, "Was the war in vain?" (61).

For Susie King Taylor, the war would not be in vain if America honored its covenant with those brave Union men who fought and died to keep the country free. She also pointedly reminded readers that "noble women as well" contributed to Civil War victory and deserved their country's gratitude (68). Her book attests not only to the deeds of valor and glory performed by enlisted men but also to the ranks of African American women who joined the campaign to create a better path to greatness, forever free of slavery.

The choices facing Susie King Taylor may have been limited by the constraints of race, gender, and region, but the heroism she demonstrated during wartime led to a lifelong vocation to keep the memories alive. She offered stirring reflections aimed at future generations. Although she died alone and unheralded in 1912, Susie King Taylor's hopes for justice live on with her memoir.

NOTES

1. See David Traxel, *1898: The Birth of the American Century* (New York: Knopf, 1998), 144, and David Blight, *Race and Reunion: The Civil War in American Memory* (Cambridge, Mass.: Harvard University Press, 2001).

2. See Blight, *Race and Reunion*, especially chapter 5, "Soldiers' Memory."

3. See Catherine Clinton, *Tara Revisited: Women, War, and the Plantation Legend* (New York: Abbeville, 1995), especially chapter 7, "The Road to Tara."

4. Blight, *Race and Reunion*, 231–37.

5. See Higginson, *The Complete Civil War Journal and Selected Letters of Thomas Wentworth Higginson*, ed. Christopher Looby (Chicago: University of Chicago Press, 2000), and chapter 7 in Edmund Wilson's *Patriotic Gore: Studies in the Literature of the American Civil War* (New York: Oxford University Press, 1962).

6. There is an extensive literature on this material. An excellent introduction to the subject is provided by Charles Davis and Henry Louis Gates Jr., *The Slave's Narrative* (New York: Oxford University Press, 1985); Marion Wilson Starling, *The Slave Narrative: Its Place in American History* (Boston: G. K. Hall, 1981); and William L. Andrews, *"To Tell a Free Story": The First Century of Afro-American Autobiography, 1760–1865* (Urbana: University of Illinois Press, 1986).

7. See George P. Rawick, ed., *The American Slave: A Composite Autobiography* (Westport, Conn.: Greenwood, 1972). See also B. A. Botkin, ed., *Lay My Burden Down: A Folk History of Slavery* (Chicago: University of Chicago Press, 1945); C. Vann Woodward, "History from Slave Sources," *American Historical Review* 79 (1974): 470–81; and Paul D. Escott, *Slavery Remembered: A Record of Twentieth-Century Slave Narratives* (Chapel Hill: University of North Carolina Press, 1979).

8. See, for example, James Henry Gooding, *On the Altar of Freedom: A Black Soldier's Civil War Letters from the Front*, ed. Virginia Matzke Adams (Amherst: University of Massachusetts Press, 1991).

9. See Charlotte L. Forten, *The Journals of Charlotte Forten*

Grimké, ed. Brenda Stevenson (New York: Oxford University Press, 1988).

10. Elizabeth Keckley, *Behind the Scenes, or, Thirty Years a Slave, and Four Years in the White House* (New York: Oxford University Press, 1988; reprint, New York: Penguin, 2005). In *Mrs. Lincoln and Mrs. Keckly: The Remarkable Story of the Friendship between a First Lady and a Former Slave* (New York: Broadway Books, 2003), Jennifer Fleischner has demonstrated that Keckly's book was published with a misspelling of her name.

11. See *The Schomburg Library of Nineteenth-Century Black Women Writers*, 40 vols., Henry Louis Gates Jr., General Editor (New York: Oxford University Press, 1988–1991).

12. See especially Catherine Clinton and Nina Silber, eds., *Divided Houses: Gender and the Civil War* (New York: Oxford University Press, 1992) and *Battle Scars: Gender and Sexuality in the American Civil War* (New York: Oxford University Press, 2006).

13. For a broader perspective on women nurses, see Jane E. Schultz, *Women at the Front: Hospital Workers in Civil War America* (Chapel Hill: University of North Carolina Press, 2004). See also Jeanie Attie, *Patriotic Toil: Northern Women and the American Civil War* (Ithaca, N.Y.: Cornell University Press, 1998).

14. See pages 29–30 of this book. All future citations to this source will be inserted parenthetically in the text.

15. Indeed, the discovery of two journals of ex-slaves who joined the Union military during the Civil War made the front page of the *New York Times*. David Blight is editing a volume that includes these previously unknown narratives. See Randy Kennedy, "Journals of Two Former Slaves Draw Vivid Portraits," 14 June 2004, *New York Times*.

16. Many scholars have dubbed this era the "nadir" of American race relations. See Rayford Logan, *The Negro in American Life and Thought: The Nadir, 1877–1901* (New York: Dial, 1954).

17. See Kenneth W. Goings, *Mammy and Uncle Mose* (Bloomington: Indiana University Press, 1994), and M. M. Manring, *Slave in a Box: The Strange Career of Aunt Jemima* (Charlottesville: University of Virginia Press, 1998).

18. See Ira Berlin, *Generations of Captivity: A History of African*

American Slaves (Cambridge, Mass.: Harvard University Press, 2003).

19. Samuel Ringgold Ward, *Autobiography of a Fugitive Negro: His Anti-slavery Labours in the United States, Canada & England* (London: John Snow, 1855), 4.

20. All information about Taylor's ancestors and family members has been derived from her own published recollections.

21. On status of hired slaves, see Timothy James Lockley, *Lines in the Sand: Race and Class in Lowcountry Georgia, 1750–1860* (Athens: University of Georgia Press, 2001), 64–66.

22. On domestic slave trade, see Julia Floyd Smith, *Slavery and Rice Culture in Low Country Georgia, 1750–1860* (Knoxville: University of Tennessee Press, 1985), 105–7.

23. Jacqueline Jones, *Soldiers of Light and Love: Northern Teachers and Georgia Blacks, 1865–1873* (Chapel Hill: University of North Carolina Press, 1980), 60; Whittington B. Johnson, *Black Savannah, 1788–1864* (Fayetteville: University of Arkansas Press, 1996), 126–29.

24. Johnson, *Black Savannah*, 127.

25. Ibid., 53.

26. Ibid., 128.

27. Ibid., 15.

28. Ibid., 25.

29. Lockley, *Lines in the Sand*, 41–43.

30. See Russell Duncan, *Freedom's Shore: Tunis Campbell and the Georgia Freedmen* (Athens: University of Georgia Press, 1986), 20–21.

31. *Christian Recorder*, 21 December 1861.

32. Katharine M. Jones, *Port Royal under Six Flags* (Indianapolis, Ind.: Bobbs-Merrill, 1960), 247.

33. For an excellent analysis, see Willie Lee Rose, *Rehearsal for Reconstruction: The Port Royal Experiment* (Indianapolis, Ind.: Bobbs-Merrill, 1964; reprint, Athens: University of Georgia Press, 1999).

34. Frederick Douglass, *The Life and Writings of Frederick Douglass*, ed. Philip S. Foner (New York: International Publishers, 1950–75), 3:365. See also James M. McPherson, *Marching toward Freedom: Blacks in the Civil War, 1861–1865* (New York: Facts on

File, 1991), and Jim Cullen, "'I'se a Man Now': Gender and African American Men," in *Divided Houses: Gender and the Civil War*, ed. Catherine Clinton and Nina Silber (New York: Oxford University Press, 1992).

35. See Edward A. Miller Jr., *Lincoln's Abolitionist General: The Biography of David Hunter* (Columbia: University of South Carolina Press, 1997).

36. General Orders No. 11, 9 May 1862, Department of the South, *The War of the Rebellion: A Compilation of the Official Records of the Union and Confederate Armies*, 6:224, 240, 14:341.

37. McPherson, *Marching toward Freedom*, 25–26.

38. For descriptions of these festivities, see Elizabeth Ware Pearson, ed., *Letters from Port Royal, 1862–1868* (1906; reprint, New York: Arno, 1969), 130, and Higginson, *The Complete Civil War Journal and Selected Letters of Thomas Wentworth Higginson*, 76–77.

39. By war's end, of the 258,000 dead Confederate soldiers, 94,000 were attributed to deaths in battle and from battle-related incidents, while 164,000 were caused by disease. Comparable Union numbers were 359,000 dead: 110,000 deaths in battle, 224,000 from disease (the remaining 25,000 were chalked up to suicides and accidents among federal troops). See Stewart Brooks, *Civil War Medicine* (Springfield, Ill.: Charles Thomas, 1966).

40. Ira Berlin et al., eds., *Freedom: A Documentary History of Emancipation, 1861–1867*, Series 2: *The Black Military Experience* (Cambridge: Cambridge University Press, 1982), 633.

41. Again, although Susie King Taylor was the only black woman nurse to leave a memoir, the published recollections of many Civil War nurses give insight into this chapter of Civil War skill and sacrifice: Hannah Ropes, *Civil War Nurse: The Diary and Letters of Hannah Ropes*, ed. John R. Brumgardt (Knoxville: University of Tennessee Press, 1980); Sophronia E. Bucklin, *In Hospital and Camp* (Philadelphia: John E. Potter, 1869); Mrs. Governor Harvey, *My Story of War: A Woman's Narrative of Life and Work in Union Hospitals* (New York: Longmans, Green, 1885); Anna Morris Ellis Holstein, *Three Years in Field Hospitals of the Army of the Potomac* (Philadelphia: J. B. Lippincott, 1867); Mary A. Livermore, *My Story of the War: A Woman's Narrative of Four Year's Personal Experience* (Hartford: A.

D. Worthington, c. 1887); *The Journals of Louisa May Alcott*, ed. Joel Myerson and Daniel Shealy (Boston: Little Brown, 1989; reprint, Athens: University of Georgia Press, 1997); Katharine Prescott Wormeley, *The Cruel Side of War: Letters from the Headquarters of the United States Sanitary Commission during the Peninsular Campaign in Virginia in 1862* (Boston: Roberts Brothers, 1898); Phoebe Yates Pember, *A Southern Woman's Story*, ed. George C. Rable (Columbia: University of South Carolina Press, 2002); and Kate Cumming, *Kate: The Journal of a Confederate Nurse*, ed. Richard Barksdale Harwell (Baton Rouge: Louisiana State University Press, 1959).

42. Stephen B. Oates, *A Woman of Valor: Clara Barton and the Civil War* (New York: Free Press, 1994), 155.

43. Ibid. Susie King Taylor took note of her meeting with Barton, but Barton did not take note of her encounter with the young black nurse.

44. Russell Duncan, *Where Death and Glory Meet: Colonel Robert Gould Shaw and the 54th Massachusetts Infantry* (Athens: University of Georgia Press, 1999).

45. Joseph T. Glatthaar, *Forged in Battle: The Civil War Alliance of Black Soldiers and White Officers* (New York: Free Press, 1990), 137–40.

46. Stephen R. Wise, *Gate of Hell: Campaign for Charleston Harbor, 1863* (Columbia: University of South Carolina Press, 1994), 113.

47. Ibid.

48. See Thomas J. Brown, Martin H. Blatt, and Donald Yacovone, eds., *Hope and Glory: Essays on the Legacy of the 54th Massachusetts Regiment* (Amherst: University of Massachusetts Press, 2001).

49. See Glatthaar, *Forged in Battle*, 140, 152.

50. See Eric Foner, *Reconstruction: America's Unfinished Revolution, 1863–1877* (New York: Harper and Row, 1988).

51. See Jacqueline Jones, *Soldiers of Light and Love: Northern Teachers and Georgia Blacks, 1865–1873* (Chapel Hill: University of North Carolina Press, 1980).

52. Ibid., 73.

53. Donald L. Grant, *The Way It Was in the South: The Black*

Experience in Georgia (Secaucus, N.J.: Carol Publishing Group, 1993; reprint, Athens: University of Georgia Press, 2001), 223.

54. See Nell Irvin Painter, *The Exodusters: Black Migration to Kansas after Reconstruction* (New York: Knopf, 1976).

55. Dorothy Sterling, *The Making of an Afro-American: Martin Robison Delany, 1812–1885* (Garden City, N.Y.: Doubleday, 1971).

SUGGESTED FURTHER READING

PRIMARY SOURCES

Forten, Charlotte L. *The Journals of Charlotte Forten Grimké.* Edited by Brenda Stevenson. New York: Oxford University Press, 1988.

Gooding, James Henry. *On the Altar of Freedom: A Black Soldier's Civil War Letters from the Front.* Edited by Virginia Matzke Adams. Amherst: University of Massachusetts Press, 1991.

Higginson, Thomas Wentworth. *The Complete Civil War Journal and Selected Letters of Thomas Wentworth Higginson.* Edited by Christopher Looby. Chicago: University of Chicago Press, 2000.

Keckley, Elizabeth. *Behind the Scenes, or, Thirty Years a Slave, and Four Years in the White House.* New York: Oxford University Press, 1988; reprint, New York: Penguin, 2005.

Pearson, Elizabeth Ware, ed. *Letters from Port Royal, 1862–1868.* 1906; reprint, New York: Arno, 1969.

Pember, Phoebe Yates. *A Southern Woman's Story.* Edited by George Rable. Columbia: University of South Carolina Press, 2002.

Rawick, George P., ed. *The American Slave: A Composite Autobiography.* Westport, Conn.: Greenwood, 1972.

Ropes, Hannah. *Civil War Nurse: The Diary and Letters of Hannah Ropes.* Edited by John R. Brumgardt. Knoxville: University of Tennessee Press, 1980.

SECONDARY SOURCES

Andrews, William L. *"To Tell a Free Story": The First Century of Afro-American Autobiography, 1760–1865.* Urbana: University of Illinois Press, 1986.

Attie, Jeanie. *Patriotic Toil: Northern Women and the American Civil War*. Ithaca, N.Y.: Cornell University Press, 1998.

Berlin, Ira, et al., eds. *Freedom: A Documentary History of Emancipation, 1861–1867*. Series 2: *The Black Military Experience*. Cambridge: Cambridge University Press, 1982.

Blight, David. *Race and Reunion: The Civil War in American Memory*. Cambridge, Mass: Harvard University Press, 2001.

Clinton, Catherine. *Harriet Tubman: The Road to Freedom*. Boston, Mass.: Little, Brown, 2004.

Clinton, Catherine, and Nina Silber, eds. *Divided Houses: Gender and the Civil War*. New York: Oxford University Press, 1992.

Escott, Paul D. *Slavery Remembered: A Record of Twentieth-Century Slave Narratives*. Chapel Hill: University of North Carolina Press, 1979.

Foner, Eric. *Reconstruction: America's Unfinished Revolution, 1863–1877*. New York: Harper and Row, 1988.

Glatthaar, Joseph. *Forged in Battle: The Civil War Alliance of Black Soldiers and White Officers*. New York: Free Press, 1990.

Johnson, Whittington B. *Black Savannah, 1788–1864*. Fayetteville: University of Arkansas Press, 1996.

Jones, Jacqueline. *Soldiers of Light and Love: Northern Teachers and Georgia Blacks, 1865–1873*. Chapel Hill: University of North Carolina Press, 1980.

Jones, Katharine M. *Port Royal under Six Flags*. Indianapolis, Ind.: Bobbs-Merrill, 1960.

Lockley, Timothy James. *Lines in the Sand: Race and Class in Lowcountry Georgia, 1750–1860*. Athens: University of Georgia Press, 2001.

Oates, Stephen B. *A Woman of Valor: Clara Barton and the Civil War*. New York: Free Press, 1994.

Rose, Willie Lee. *Rehearsal for Reconstruction: The Port Royal Experiment*. Indianapolis, Ind.: Bobbs-Merrill, 1964; reprint, Athens: University of Georgia Press, 1999.

Schultz, Jane E. *Women at the Front: Hospital Workers in Civil War America*. Chapel Hill: University of North Carolina Press, 2004.

Smith, Julia Floyd. *Slavery and Rice Culture in Low Country Georgia, 1750–1860*. Knoxville: University of Tennessee Press, 1985.

Wood, Betty. *Gender, Race and Rank in a Revolutionary Age: The Georgia Lowcountry, 1750–1820*. Athens: University of Georgia Press, 2000.

———. *Women's Work, Men's Work: The Informal Slave Economies of Lowcountry Georgia*. Athens: University of Georgia Press, 1995.

REMINISCENCES
OF MY LIFE IN CAMP

To

COLONEL T. W. HIGGINSON

THESE PAGES
ARE GRATEFULLY DEDICATED

LETTER FROM COL. C. T. TROWBRIDGE

St. Paul, Minn., April 7, 1902.

Mrs. Susan King Taylor:

Dear Madam, — The manuscript of the story of your army life reached me to-day. I have read it with much care and interest, and I most willingly and cordially indorse it as a truthful account of your unselfish devotion and service through more than three long years of war in which the 33d Regiment bore a conspicuous part in the great conflict for human liberty and the restoration of the Union. I most sincerely regret that through a technicality you are debarred from having your name placed on the roll of pensioners, as an Army Nurse; for among all the number of heroic women whom the government is now rewarding, I know of no one more deserving than yourself.

Yours in F. C. & L.,

C. T. TROWBRIDGE,
Late Lt.-Col. 33d U. S. C. T.

PREFACE

I HAVE been asked many times by my friends,
and also by members of the Grand Army of the
Republic and Women's Relief Corps, to write a
book of my army life, during the war of 1861–65,
with the regiment of the 1st South Carolina
Colored Troops, later called 33d United States
Colored Infantry.

At first I did not think I would, but as the
years rolled on and my friends were still urging
me to start with it, I wrote to Colonel C. T.
Trowbridge (who had command of this regiment), asking his opinion and advice on the matter. His answer to me was, "Go ahead! write
it; that is just what I should do, were I in your
place, and I will give you all the assistance you
may need, whenever you require it." This in-
spired me very much.

In 1900 I received a letter from a gentleman,
sent from the Executive Mansion at St. Paul,
Minn., saying Colonel Trowbridge had told him
I was about to write a book, and when it was

published he wanted one of the first copies. This, coming from a total stranger, gave me more confidence, so I now present these reminiscences to you, hoping they may prove of some interest, and show how much service and good we can do to each other, and what sacrifices we can make for our liberty and rights, and that there were "loyal women," as well as men, in those days, who did not fear shell or shot, who cared for the sick and dying; women who camped and fared as the boys did, and who are still caring for the comrades in their declining years.

So, with the hope that the following pages will accomplish some good and instruction for its readers, I shall proceed with my narrative.

SUSIE KING TAYLOR.

Boston, 1902.

INTRODUCTION

ACTUAL military life is rarely described by a
woman, and this is especially true of a woman
whose place was in the ranks, as the wife of a
soldier and herself a regimental laundress. No
such description has ever been given, I am sure,
by one thus connected with a colored regiment;
so that the nearly 200,000 black soldiers (178,-
975) of our Civil War have never before been
delineated from the woman's point of view. All
this gives peculiar interest to this little volume,
relating wholly to the career of the very earliest
of these regiments, — the one described by myself, from a wholly different point of view, in
my volume " Army Life in a Black Regiment,"
long since translated into French by the Com-
tesse de Gasparin under the title " Vie Militaire
dans un Régiment Noir."

The writer of the present book was very exceptional among the colored laundresses, in that she
could read and write and had taught children to
do the same ; and her whole life and career were

most estimable, both during the war and in the later period during which she has lived in Boston and has made many friends. I may add that I did not see the book until the sheets were in print, and have left it wholly untouched, except as to a few errors in proper names. I commend the narrative to those who love the plain record of simple lives, led in stormy periods.

THOMAS WENTWORTH HIGGINSON,

Former Colonel 1st S. C. Volunteers
(afterwards 33d U. S. Colored Infantry).

CAMBRIDGE, MASS.,
November 3, 1902.

REMINISCENCES

I

A BRIEF SKETCH OF MY ANCESTORS

My great-great-grandmother was 120 years old when she died. She had seven children, and five of her boys were in the Revolutionary War. She was from Virginia, and was half Indian. She was so old she had to be held in the sun to help restore or prolong her vitality.

My great-grandmother, one of her daughters, named Susanna, was married to Peter Simons, and was one hundred years old when she died, from a stroke of paralysis in Savannah. She was the mother of twenty-four children, twenty-three being girls. She was one of the noted midwives of her day. In 1820 my grandmother was born, and named after her grandmother, Dolly, and in 1833 she married Fortune Lambert Reed. Two children blessed their union, James and Hagar Ann. James died at the age of twelve years.

My mother was born in 1834. She married
Raymond Baker in 1847. Nine children were
born to them, three dying in infancy. I was the
first born. I was born on the Grest Farm (which
was on an island known as Isle of Wight), Liberty County, about thirty-five miles from Savannah, Ga., on August 6, 1848, my mother being
waitress for the Grest family. I have often been
told by mother of the care Mrs. Grest took of
me. She was very fond of me, and I remember
when my brother and I were small children, and
Mr. Grest would go away on business, Mrs.
Grest would place us at the foot of her bed to
sleep and keep her company. Sometimes he
would return home earlier than he had expected
to ; then she would put us on the floor.

When I was about seven years old, Mr. Grest
allowed my grandmother to take my brother and
me to live with her in Savannah. There were no
railroad connections in those days between this
place and Savannah; all travel was by stage-
coaches. I remember, as if it were yesterday,
the coach which ran in from Savannah, with its
driver, whose beard nearly reached his knees.
His name was Shakespeare, and often I would go
to the stable where he kept his horses, on Barnard Street in front of the old Arsenal, just to
look at his wonderful beard.

My grandmother went every three months to
see my mother. She would hire a wagon to carry

bacon, tobacco, flour, molasses, and sugar. These she would trade with people in the neighboring places, for eggs, chickens, or cash, if they had it. These, in turn, she carried back to the city market, where she had a customer who sold them for her. The profit from these, together with laundry work and care. of some bachelors' rooms, made a good living for her.

The hardest blow to her was the failure of the Freedmen's Savings Bank in Savannah, for in that bank she had placed her savings, about three thousand dollars, the result of her hard labor and self-denial before the war, and which, by dint of shrewdness and care, she kept together all through the war. She felt it more keenly, coming as it did in her old age, when her life was too far spent to begin anew ; but she took a practical view of the matter, for she said, " I will leave it all in God's hand. If the Yankees did take all our money, they freed my race ; God will take care of us."

In 1888 she wrote me here (Boston), asking me to visit her, as she was getting very feeble and wanted to see me once before she passed away. I made up my mind to leave at once, but about the time I planned to go, in March, a fearful blizzard swept our country, and travel was at a standstill for nearly two weeks ; but March 15 I left on the first through steamer from New York, en route for the South, where I again saw my grandmother, and we felt thankful that we were spared to meet each other once more. This was the last time I saw her, for in May, 1889, she died.

II

I WAS born under the slave law in Georgia, in 1848, and was brought up by my grandmother in Savannah. There were three of us with her, my younger sister and brother. My brother and I being the two eldest, we were sent to a friend of my grandmother, Mrs. Woodhouse, a widow, to learn to read and write. She was a free woman and lived on Bay Lane, between Habersham and Price streets, about half a mile from my house. We went every day about nine o'clock, with our books wrapped in paper to prevent the police or white persons from seeing them. We went in, one at a time, through the gate, into the yard to the L kitchen, which was the schoolroom. She had twenty-five or thirty children whom she taught, assisted by her daughter, Mary Jane. The neighbors would see us going in sometimes, but they supposed we were there learning trades, as it was the custom to give children a trade of some kind. After school we left the same way we entered, one by one, when we would go to a square, about a block from the school, and wait for each other. We would gather laurel leaves and pop them on our hands, on our way home. I remained at her school for two years or more, when I was sent to a Mrs. Mary Beasley, where I continued until May, 1860, when she told my grandmother she had taught me all she knew, and grandmother had better get some one else who could teach me more, so I stopped my studies for a while.

I had a white playmate about this time, named Katie O'Connor, who lived on the next corner of the street from my house, and who attended a convent. One day she told me, if I would promise not to tell her father, she would give me some lessons. On my promise not to do so, and getting her mother's consent, she gave me lessons about four months, every evening. At the end of this time she was put into the convent permanently, and I have never seen her since.

A month after this, James Blouis, our landlord's son, was attending the High School, and was very fond of grandmother, so she asked him to give me a few lessons, which he did until the middle of 1861, when the Savannah Volunteer Guards, to which he and his brother belonged, were ordered to the front under General Barton. In the first battle of Manassas, his brother Eugene was killed, and James deserted over to the Union side, and at the close of the war went to Washington, D. C., where he has since resided.

I often wrote passes for my grandmother, for all colored persons, free or slaves, were compelled to have a pass; free colored people having a guardian in place of a master. These passes were good until 10 or 10.30 P. M. for one night or every night for one month. The pass read as follows: —

SAVANNAH, GA., March 1st, 1860.

Pass the bearer —————— from 9 to 10.30. P. M.

VALENTINE GREST.

Every person had to have this pass, for at nine o'clock each night a bell was rung, and any colored persons found on the street after this hour were arrested by the watchman, and put in the guard-house until next morning, when their owners would pay their fines and release them. I knew a number of persons who went out at any time at night and were never arrested, as the watchman knew them so well he never stopped them, and seldom asked to see their passes, only stopping them long enough, sometimes, to say "Howdy," and then telling them to go along.

About this time I had been reading so much about the "Yankees" I was very anxious to see them. The whites would tell their colored people not to go to the Yankees, for they would harness them to carts and make them pull the carts around, in place of horses. I asked grandmother, one day, if this was true. She replied, "Cer-

tainly not!'" that the white people did not want
slaves to go over to the Yankees, and told them
these things to frighten them. " Don't you see
those signs pasted about the streets? one reading,
'I am a rattlesnake; if you touch me I will
strike!' Another reads, 'I am a wild-cat! Be-
ware,' etc. These are warnings to the North; so
don't mind what the white people say." I wanted
to see these wonderful " Yankees " so much, as I
heard my parents say the Yankee was going to
set all the slaves free. Oh, how those people
prayed for freedom! I remember, one night,
my grandmother went out into the suburbs of the
city to a church meeting, and they were fervently
singing this old hymn, —

> "Yes, we all shall be free,
> Yes, we all shall be free,
> Yes, we all shall be free,
> When the Lord shall appear," —

when the police came in and arrested all who were
there, saying they were planning freedom, and
sang " the Lord," in place of " Yankee," to blind
any one who might be listening. Grandmother
never forgot that night, although she did not stay
in the guard-house, as she sent to her guardian,
who came at once for her; but this was the last
meeting she ever attended out of the city proper.

On April 1, 1862, about the time the Union
soldiers were firing on Fort Pulaski, I was sent
out into the country to my mother. I remember

what a roar and din the guns made. They jarred
the earth for miles. The fort was at last taken
by them. Two days after the taking of Fort
Pulaski, my uncle took his family of seven and
myself to St. Catherine Island. We landed under
the protection of the Union fleet, and remained
there two weeks, when about thirty of us were
taken aboard the gunboat P———, to be transferred to St. Simon's Island; and at last, to my
unbounded joy, I saw the "Yankee."

After we were all settled aboard and started on
our journey, Captain Whitmore, commanding the
boat, asked me where I was from. I told him
Savannah, Ga. He asked if I could read; I said,
"Yes!" "Can you write?" he next asked. "Yes,
I can do that also," I replied, and as if he had
some doubts of my answers he handed me a book
and a pencil and told me to write my name and
where I was from. I did this; when he wanted
to know if I could sew. On hearing I could, he
asked me to hem some napkins for him. He was
surprised at my accomplishments (for they were
such in those days), for he said he did not know
there were any negroes in the South able to read
or write. He said, "You seem to be so different
from the other colored people who came from the
same place you did." "No!" I replied, "the
only difference is, they were reared in the country and I in the city, as was a man from Darien,
Ga., named Edward King." That seemed to

satisfy him, and we had no further conversation that day on the subject.

In the afternoon the captain spied a boat in the distance, and as it drew nearer he noticed it had a white flag hoisted, but before it had reached the Putumoka he ordered all passengers between decks, so we could not be seen, for he thought they might be spies. The boat finally drew alongside of our boat, and had Mr. Edward Donegall on board, who wanted his two servants, Nick and Judith. He wanted these, as they were his own children. Our captain told him he knew nothing of them, which was true, for at the time they were on St. Simon's, and not, as their father supposed, on our boat. After the boat left, we were allowed to come up on deck again.

III

NEXT morning we arrived at St. Simon's, and the captain told Commodore Goldsborough about this affair, and his reply was, "Captain Whitmore, you should not have allowed them to return; you should have kept them." After I had been on St. Simon's about three days, Commodore Goldsborough heard of me, and came to Gaston Bluff to see me. I found him very cordial. He said Captain Whitmore had spoken to him of me, and that he was pleased to hear of my being so capable, etc., and wished me to take charge of a school for the children on the island. I told him I would gladly do so, if I could have some books. He said I should have them, and in a week or two I received two large boxes of books and testaments from the North. I had about forty children to teach, beside a number of adults who came to me nights, all of them so eager to learn to read, to read above anything else. Chaplain French, of Boston, would come to the school, sometimes, and lecture to the pupils on Boston and the North.

About the first of June we were told that there

was going to be a settlement of the war. Those
who were on the Union side would remain free,
and those in bondage were to work three days for
their masters and three for themselves. It was
a gloomy time for us all, and we were to be sent
to Liberia. Chaplain French asked me would I
rather go back to Savannah or go to Liberia. I
told him the latter place by all means. We did
not know when this would be, but we were prepared in case this settlement should be reached.
However, the Confederates would not agree to the
arrangement, or else it was one of the many
rumors flying about at the time, as we heard nothing further of the matter. There were a number of settlements on this island of St. Simon's,
just like little villages, and we would go from one
to the other on business, to call, or only for a
walk.

One Sunday, two men, Adam Miller and Daniel
Spaulding, were chased by some rebels as they
were coming from Hope Place (which was between the Beach and Gaston Bluff), but the latter
were unable to catch them. When they reached
the Beach and told this, all the men on the place,
about ninety, armed themselves, and next day
(Monday), with Charles O'Neal as their leader,
skirmished the island for the "rebs." In a short
while they discovered them in the woods, hidden
behind a large log, among the thick underbrush.
Charles O'Neal was the first to see them, and he

was killed; also John Brown, and their bodies
were never found.   Charles O'Neal was an uncle
of Edward King, who later was my husband and
a sergeant in Co. E., U. S. I.   Another man was
shot, but not found for three days.   On Tuesday,
the second day, Captain Trowbridge and some
soldiers landed, and assisted the skirmishers.
Word having been sent by the mail-boat Uncas
to Hilton Head, later in the day Commodore
Goldsborough, who was in command of the naval
station, landed about three hundred marines, and
joined the others to oust the rebels.   On Wednes-
day, John Baker, the man shot on Monday, was
found in a terrible condition by Henry Batchlott,
who carried him to the Beach, where he was attended by the surgeon.   He told us how, after being shot, he lay quiet for a day.   On the second
day he managed to reach some wild grapes growing near him.   These he ate, to satisfy his hunger
and intense thirst, then he crawled slowly, every
movement causing agony, until he got to the side
of the road.   He lived only three months after
they found him.

On the second day of the skirmish the troops
captured a boat which they knew the Confederates
had used to land in, and having this in their possession, the " rebs " could not return; so pickets
were stationed all around the island.   There was
an old man, Henry Capers, who had been left on
one of the places by his old master, Mr. Hazzard,

as he was too old to carry away. These rebels
went to his house in the night, and he hid them
up in the loft. On Tuesday all hands went to
this man's house with a determination to burn it
down, but Henry Batchlott pleaded with the men
to spare it. The rebels were in hiding, still, waiting a chance to get off the island. They searched
his house, but neglected to go up into the loft,
and in so doing missed the rebels concealed there.
Late in the night Henry Capers gave them his
boat to escape in, and they got off all right. This
old man was allowed by the men in charge of the
island to cut grass for his horse, and to have a
boat to carry this grass to his home, and so they
were not detected, our men thinking it was Capers
using the boat. After Commodore Goldsborough
left the island, Commodore Judon sent the old
man over to the mainland and would not allow
him to remain on the island.

There were about six hundred men, women,
and children on St. Simon's, the women and children being in the majority, and we were afraid to
go very far from our own quarters in the day-
time, and at night even to go out of the house
for a long time, although the men were on the
watch all the time ; for there were not any soldiers
on the island, only the marines who were on the
gunboats along the coast. The rebels, knowing
this, could steal by them under cover of the night,
and getting on the island would capture any per-

sons venturing out alone and carry them to the mainland. Several of the men disappeared, and as they were never heard from we came to the conclusion they had been carried off in this way.

The latter part of August, 1862, Captain C. T. Trowbridge, with his brother John and Lieutenant Walker, came to St. Simon's Island from Hilton Head, by order of General Hunter, to get all the men possible to finish filling his regiment which he had organized in March, 1862. He had heard of the skirmish on this island, and was very much pleased at the bravery shown by these men. He found me at Gaston Bluff teaching my little school, and was much interested in it. When I knew him better I found him to be a thorough gentleman and a staunch friend to my race.

Captain Trowbridge remained with us until October, when the order was received to evacuate, and so we boarded the Ben-De-Ford, a transport, for Beaufort, S. C. When we arrived in Beaufort, Captain Trowbridge and the men he had enlisted went to camp at Old Fort, which they named "Camp Saxton." I was enrolled as laundress.

The first suits worn by the boys were red coats and pants, which they disliked very much, for, they said, "The rebels see us, miles away."

The first colored troops did not receive any pay for eighteen months, and the men had to depend wholly on what they received from the commissary, established by General Saxton. A great many of these men had large families, and as they had no money to give them, their wives were obliged to support themselves and children by washing for the officers of the gunboats and the soldiers, and making cakes and pies which they sold to the boys in camp. Finally, in 1863, the government decided to give them half pay, but the men would not accept this. They wanted "full pay" or nothing. They preferred rather to give their services to the state, which they did until 1864, when the government granted them full pay, with all the back pay due.

I remember hearing Captain Heasley telling his company, one day, "Boys, stand up for your full pay! I am with you, and so are all the officers." This captain was from Pennsylvania, and was a very good man; all the men liked him. N. G. Parker, our first lieutenant, was from Massachusetts. H. A. Beach was from New York. He was very delicate, and had to resign in 1864 on account of ill health.

I had a number of relatives in this regiment, — several uncles, some cousins, and a husband in Company E, and a number of cousins in other companies. Major Strong, of this regiment, started home on a furlough, but the vessel he was aboard was lost, and he never reached his home. He was one of the best officers we had. After his death, Captain C. T. Trowbridge was promoted major, August, 1863, and filled Major Strong's place until December, 1864, when he was promoted lieutenant-colonel, which he remained until he was mustered out, February 6, 1866.

In February, 1863, several cases of varioloid broke out among the boys, which caused some anxiety in camp. Edward Davis, of Company E (the company I was with), had it very badly. He was put into a tent apart from the rest of the men, and only the doctor and camp steward, James Cummings, were allowed to see or attend him; but I went to see this man every day and nursed him. The last thing at night, I always went in to see that he was comfortable, but in spite of the good care and attention he received, he succumbed to the disease.

I was not in the least afraid of the small-pox. I had been vaccinated, and I drank sassafras tea constantly, which kept my blood purged and prevented me from contracting this dread scourge, and no one need fear getting it if they will only keep their blood in good condition with this sassafras tea, and take it before going where the patient is.

IV

On the first of January, 1863, we held services for the purpose of listening to the reading of President Lincoln's proclamation by Dr. W. H. Brisbane, and the presentation of two beautiful stands of colors, one from a lady in Connecticut, and the other from Rev. Mr. Cheever. The presentation speech was made by Chaplain French. It was a glorious day for us all, and we enjoyed every minute of it, and as a fitting close and the crowning event of this occasion we had a grand barbecue. A number of oxen were roasted whole, and we had a fine feast. Although not served as tastily or correctly as it would have been at home, yet it was enjoyed with keen appetites and relish. The soldiers had a good time. They sang or shouted "Hurrah!" all through the camp, and seemed overflowing with fun and frolic until taps were sounded, when many, no doubt, dreamt of this memorable day.

I had rather an amusing experience; that is, it seems amusing now, as I look back, but at the time it occurred it was a most serious one to me.

When our regiment left Beaufort for Seabrooke, I left some of my things with a neighbor who lived outside of the camp. After I had been at Seabrooke about a week, I decided to return to Camp Saxton and get them. So one morning, with Mary Shaw, a friend who was in the company at that time, I started off. There was no way for us to get to Beaufort other than to walk, except we rode on the commissary wagon. This we did, and reached Beaufort about one o'clock. We then had more than two miles to walk before reaching our old camp, and expected to be able to accomplish this and return in time to meet the wagon again by three o'clock that afternoon, and so be taken back. We failed to do this, however, for when we got to Beaufort the wagon was gone. We did not know what to do. I did not wish to remain overnight, neither did my friend, although we might easily have stayed, as both had relatives in the town.

It was in the springtime, and the days were long, and as the sun looked so bright, we concluded to walk back, thinking we should reach camp before dark. So off we started on our ten-mile tramp. We had not gone many miles, however, before we were all tired out and began to regret our undertaking. The sun was getting low, and we grew more frightened, fearful of meeting some animal or of treading on a snake on our way. We did not meet a person, and we

were frightened almost to death. Our feet were
so sore we could hardly walk. Finally we took
off our shoes and tried walking in our stocking
feet, but this made them worse. We had gone
about six miles when night overtook us. There
we were, nothing around us but dense woods, and
as there was no house or any place to stop at,
there was nothing for us to do but continue on.
We were afraid to speak to each other.

Meantime at the camp, seeing no signs of us
by dusk, they concluded we had decided to remain over until next day, and so had no idea of
our plight. Imagine their surprise when we
reached camp about eleven P. M. The guard
challenged us, " Who comes there ? " My answer was, " A friend without a countersign." He
approached and saw who it was, reported, and
we were admitted into the lines. They had the
joke on us that night, and for a long time after
would tease us ; and sometimes some of the men
who were on guard that night would call us de-
serters. They used to laugh at us, but we joined
with them too, especially when we would tell
them our experience on our way to camp. I did
not undertake that trip again, as there was no
way of getting in or out except one took the
provision wagon, and there was not much depend-
ence to be put in that returning to camp. Perhaps the driver would say one hour and he might
be there earlier or later. Of course it was not

his fault, as it depended when the order was filled at the Commissary Department; therefore I did not go any more until the regiment was ordered to our new camp, which was named after our hero, Colonel Shaw, who at that time was at Beaufort with his regiment, the 54th Massachusetts.

I taught a great many of the comrades in Company E to read and write, when they were off duty. Nearly all were anxious to learn. My husband taught some also when it was convenient for him. I was very happy to know my efforts were successful in camp, and also felt grateful for the appreciation of my services. I gave my services willingly for four years and three months without receiving a dollar. I was glad, however, to be allowed to go with the regiment, to care for the sick and afflicted comrades.

V

In the latter part of 1862 the regiment made an expedition into Darien, Georgia, and up the Ridge, and on January 23, 1863, another up St. Mary's River, capturing a number of stores for the government; then on to Fernandina, Florida. They were gone ten or twelve days, at the end of which time they returned to camp.

March 10, 1863, we were ordered to Jacksonville, Florida. Leaving Camp Saxton between four and five o'clock, we arrived at Jacksonville about eight o'clock next morning, accompanied by three or four gunboats. When the rebels saw these boats, they ran out of the city, leaving the women behind, and we found out afterwards that they thought we had a much larger fleet than we really had. Our regiment was kept out of sight until we made fast at the wharf where it landed, and while the gunboats were shelling up the river and as far inland as possible, the regiment landed and marched up the street, where they spied the rebels who had fled from the city. They were hiding behind a house about a mile or so away, their faces blackened to disguise themselves as negroes, and our boys, as they advanced toward them, halted a second, saying, "They are black men! Let them come to us, or we will make them know who we are." With this, the firing was opened and several of our men were wounded and killed. The rebels had a number wounded and killed. It was through this way the discovery was made that they were white men. Our men drove them some distance in retreat and then threw out their pickets.

While the fighting was on, a friend, Lizzie Lancaster, and I stopped at several of the rebel homes, and after talking with some of the women and children we asked them if they had any food. They claimed to have only some hard-tack, and evidently did not care to give us anything to eat, but this was not surprising. They were bitterly against our people and had no mercy or sympathy for us.

The second day, our boys were reinforced by a regiment of white soldiers, a Maine regiment, and by cavalry, and had quite a fight. On the third day, Edward Herron, who was a fine gunner on the steamer John Adams, came on shore, bringing a small cannon, which the men pulled along for more than five miles. This cannon was the only piece for shelling. On coming upon the enemy, all secured their places, and they had a lively fight, which lasted several hours, and our boys were nearly captured by the Confederates ; but the Union boys carried out all their plans that day, and succeeded in driving the enemy back. After this skirmish, every afternoon between four and five o'clock the Confederate General Finegan would send a flag of truce to Colonel Higginson, warning him to send all women and children out of the city, and threatening to bombard it if this was not done. Our colonel allowed all to go who wished, at first, but as General Finegan grew more hostile and kept sending these communications for nearly a week, Colonel Higginson thought it not best or necessary to send any more out of the city, and so informed General Finegan. This angered the general, for that night the rebels shelled directly toward Colonel Higginson's headquarters. The shelling was so heavy that the colonel told my captain to have me taken up into the town to a hotel, which was used as a hospital. As my quarters were just in the rear of the colonel's, he was compelled to leave his also before the night was over. I expected every moment to be killed by a shell, but on arriving at the hospital I knew I was safe, for the shells could not reach us there. It was plainly to be seen now, the ruse of the flag of truce coming so often to us. The bearer was evidently a spy getting the location of the headquarters, etc., for the shells were sent too accurately to be at random.

Next morning Colonel Higginson took the cavalry and a regiment on another tramp after the rebels. They were gone several days and had the hardest fight they had had, for they wanted to go as far as a station which was some distance from the city. The gunboats were of little assistance to them, yet notwithstanding this drawback our boys returned with only a few killed and wounded, and after this we were not troubled with General Finegan.

We remained here a few weeks longer, when, about April first, the regiment was ordered back to Camp Saxton, where it stayed a week, when the order came to go to Port Royal Ferry on picket duty. It was a gay day for the boys. By seven o'clock all tents were down, and each company, with a commissary wagon, marched up the shell road, which is a beautiful avenue ten or twelve miles out of Beaufort. We arrived at Seabrooke at about four o'clock, where our tents were pitched and the men put on duty. We were here a few weeks, when Company E was ordered to Barnwell plantation for picket duty.

Some mornings I would go along the picket line, and I could see the rebels on the opposite side of the river. Sometimes as they were changing pickets they would call over to our men and ask for something to eat, or for tobacco, and our men would tell them to come over. Sometimes one or two would desert to us, saying, they "had no negroes to fight for." Others would shoot

across at our picket, but as the river was so wide
there was never any damage done, and the Confederates never attempted to shell us while we
were there.

I learned to handle a musket very well while
in the regiment, and could shoot straight and often
hit the target. I assisted in cleaning the guns
and used to fire them off, to see if the cartridges
were dry, before cleaning and reloading, each day.
I thought this great fun. I was also able to take
a gun all apart, and put it together again.

Between Barnwell and the mainland was Hall
Island. I went over there several times with Sergeant King and other comrades. One night there
was a stir in camp when it was found that the
rebels were trying to cross, and next morning
Lieutenant Parker told me he thought they were
on Hall Island; so after that I did not go over
again.

While planning for the expedition up the
Edisto River, Colonel Higginson was a whole
night in the water, trying to locate the rebels and
where their picket lines were situated. About
July the boys went up the Edisto to destroy a
bridge on the Charleston and Savannah road.
This expedition was twenty or more miles into
the mainland. Colonel Higginson was wounded
in this fight and the regiment nearly captured.
The steamboat John Adams always assisted us,
carrying soldiers, provisions, etc. She carried

several guns and a good gunner, Edward Herron.
Henry Batchlott, a relative of mine, was a steward on this boat.   There were two smaller boats,
Governor Milton and the Enoch Dean, in the
fleet, as these could go up the river better than
the larger ones could.   I often went aboard the
John Adams.   It went with us into Jacksonville,
to Cole and Folly Island, and Gunner Herron was
always ready to send a shell at the enemy.

One night, Companies K and E, on their way
to Pocotaligo to destroy a battery that was situated down the river, captured several prisoners.
The rebels nearly captured Sergeant King, who,
as he sprang and caught a "reb," fell over an
embankment.   In falling he did not release his
hold on his prisoner.   Although his hip was severely injured, he held fast until some of his comrades came to his aid and pulled them up.   These
expeditions were very dangerous.   Sometimes the
men had to go five or ten miles during the night
over on the rebel side and capture or destroy
whatever they could find.

While at Camp Shaw, there was a deserter who
came into Beaufort.   He was allowed his freedom
about the city and was not molested.   He remained about the place a little while and returned
to the rebels again.   On his return to Beaufort a
second time, he was held as a spy, tried, and sen-
tenced to death, for he was a traitor.   The day
he was shot, he was placed on a hearse with his

coffin inside, a guard was placed either side of the
hearse, and he was driven through the town.   All
the soldiers and people in town were out, as this
was to be a warning to the soldiers.   Our regiment was in line on dress parade.   They drove
with him to the rear of our camp, where he was
shot.   I shall never forget this scene.

While at Camp Shaw, Chaplain Fowler, Robert
Defoe, and several of our boys were captured
while tapping some telegraph wires.   Robert Defoe was confined in the jail at Walterborough,
S. C., for about twenty months.   When Sherman's
army reached Pocotaligo he made his escape and
joined his company (Company G).   He had not
been paid, as he had refused the reduced pay offered by the government.   Before we got to camp,
where the pay-rolls could be made out, he sickened
and died of small-pox, and was buried at Savannah, never having been paid one cent for nearly
three years of service.   He left no heirs and his
account was never settled.

In winter, when it was very cold, I would take
a mess-pan, put a little earth in the bottom, and
go to the cook-shed and fill it nearly full of coals,
carry it back to my tent and put another pan
over it; so when the provost guard went through
camp after taps, they would not see the light, as
it was against the rules to have a light after taps.
In this way I was heated and kept very warm.

A mess-pan is made of sheet iron, something

like our roasting pans, only they are nearly as large round as a peck measure, but not so deep. We had fresh beef once in a while, and we would have soup, and the vegetables they put in this soup were dried and pressed. They looked like hops. Salt beef was our stand-by. Sometimes the men would have what we called slap-jacks. This was flour, made into bread and spread thin on the bottom of the mess-pan to cook. Each man had one of them, with a pint of tea, for his supper, or a pint of tea and five or six hard-tack. I often got my own meals, and would fix some dishes for the non-commissioned officers also.

Mrs. Chamberlain, our quartermaster's wife, was with us here. She was a beautiful woman; I can see her pleasant face before me now, as she, with Captain Trowbridge, would sit and converse with me in my tent two or three hours at a time. She was also with me on Cole Island, and I think we were the only women with the regiment while there. I remember well how, when she first came into camp, Captain Trowbridge brought her to my tent and introduced her to me. I found her then, as she remained ever after, a lovely person, and I always admired her cordial and friendly ways.

Our boys would say to me sometimes, "Mrs. King, why is it you are so kind to us? you treat us just as you do the boys in your own company." I replied, " Well, you know, all the boys in other companies are the same to me as those in my Company E; you are all doing the same duty, and I will do just the same for you." " Yes," they would say, " we know that, because you were the first woman we saw when we came into camp, and you took an interest in us boys ever since we have been here, and we are very grateful for all you do for us."

When at Camp Shaw, I visited the hospital in Beaufort, where I met Clara Barton. There were a number of sick and wounded soldiers there, and I went often to see the comrades. Miss Barton was always very cordial toward me, and I honored her for her devotion and care of those men.

There was a man, John Johnson, who with his family was taken by our regiment at Edisto. This man afterwards worked in the hospital and was well known to Miss Barton. I have been told since that when she went South, in 1883, she tried to look this man up, but learned he was dead. His son is living in Edisto, Rev. J. J. Johnson, and is the president of an industrial school on that island and a very intelligent man. He was a small child when his father and family were captured by our regiment at Edisto.

VI

FORT WAGNER being only a mile from our camp,
I went there two or three times a week, and
would go up on the ramparts to watch the gunners
send their shells into Charleston (which they did
every fifteen minutes), and had a full view of the
city from that point. Outside of the fort were
many skulls lying about; I have often moved them
one side out of the path. The comrades and I
would have quite a debate as to which side the
men fought on. Some thought they were the
skulls of our boys; others thought they were the
enemy's; but as there was no definite way to
know, it was never decided which could lay claim
to them. They were a gruesome sight, those
fleshless heads and grinning jaws, but by this time
I had become accustomed to worse things and did
not feel as I might have earlier in my camp life.

It seems strange how our aversion to seeing suffering is overcome in war, — how we are able to
see the most sickening sights, such as men with
their limbs blown off and mangled by the deadly
shells, without a shudder; and instead of turning
away, how we hurry to assist in alleviating their

pain, bind up their wounds, and press the cool water to their parched lips, with feelings only of sympathy and pity.

About the first of June, 1864, the regiment was ordered to Folly Island, staying there until the latter part of the month, when it was ordered to Morris Island. We landed on Morris Island between June and July, 1864. This island was a narrow strip of sandy soil, nothing growing on it but a few bushes and shrubs. The camp was one mile from the boat landing, called Pawnell Landing, and the landing one mile from Fort Wagner.

Colonel Higginson had left us in May of this year, on account of wounds received at Edisto. All the men were sorry to lose him. They did not want him to go, they loved him so. He was kind and devoted to his men, thoughtful for their comfort, and we missed his genial presence from the camp.

The regiment under Colonel Trowbridge did garrison duty, but they had troublesome times from Fort Gregg, on James Island, for the rebels would throw a shell over on our island every now and then. Finally orders were received for the boys to prepare to take Fort Gregg, each man to take 150 rounds of cartridges, canteens of water, hard-tack, and salt beef. This order was sent three days prior to starting, to allow them to be in readiness. I helped as many as I could to pack haversacks and cartridge boxes.

The fourth day, about five o'clock in the afternoon, the call was sounded, and I heard the first sergeant say, " Fall in, boys, fall in," and they were not long obeying the command. Each company marched out of its street, in front of their colonel's headquarters, where they rested for half an hour, as it was not dark enough, and they did not want the enemy to have a chance to spy their movements. At the end of this time the line was formed with the 103d New York (white) in the rear, and off they started, eager to get to work. It was quite dark by the time they reached Pawnell Landing. I have never forgotten the goodbys of that day, as they left camp. Colonel Trowbridge said to me as he left, " Good-by, Mrs. King, take care of yourself if you don't see us again." I went with them as far as the landing, and watched them until they got out of sight, and then I returned to the camp. There was no one at camp but those left on picket and a few disabled soldiers, and one woman, a friend of mine, Mary Shaw, and it was lonesome and sad, now that the boys were gone, some never to return.

Mary Shaw shared my tent that night, and we went to bed, but not to sleep, for the fleas nearly ate us alive. We caught a few, but it did seem, now that the men were gone, that every flea in camp had located my tent, and caused us to vacate. Sleep being out of the question, we sat up the remainder of the night.

About four o'clock, July 2, the charge was
made. The firing could be plainly heard in
camp. I hastened down to the landing and remained there until eight o'clock that morning.
When the wounded arrived, or rather began to
arrive, the first one brought in was Samuel An-
derson of our company. He was badly wounded.
Then others of our boys, some with their legs off,
arm gone, foot off, and wounds of all kinds ima-
ginable. They had to wade through creeks and
marshes, as they were discovered by the enemy
and shelled very badly. A number of the men
were lost, some got fastened in the mud and had
to cut off the legs of their pants, to free themselves. The 103d New York suffered the most,
as their men were very badly wounded.

My work now began. I gave my assistance to
try to alleviate their sufferings. I asked the doctor at the hospital what I could get for them to
eat. They wanted soup, but that I could not get;
but I had a few cans of condensed milk and some
turtle eggs, so I thought I would try to make
some custard. I had doubts as to my success,
for cooking with turtle eggs was something new
to me, but the adage has it, " Nothing ventured,
nothing done," so I made a venture and the result was a very delicious custard. This I carried
to the men, who enjoyed it very much. My services were given at all times for the comfort of
these men. I was on hand to assist whenever

needed. I was enrolled as company laundress, but I did very little of it, because I was always busy doing other things through camp, and was employed all the time doing something for the officers and comrades.

After this fight, the regiment did not return to the camp for one month. They were ordered to Cole Island in September, where they remained until October. About November 1, 1864, six companies were detailed to go to Gregg Landing, Port Royal Ferry, and the rebels in some way found out some of our forces had been removed and gave our boys in camp a hard time of it, for several nights. In fact, one night it was thought the boys would have to retreat. The colonel told me to go down to the landing, and if they were obliged to retreat, I could go aboard one of our gunboats. One of the gunboats got in the rear, and began to shell General Beauregard's force, which helped our boys retain their possession.

About November 15, I received a letter from Sergeant King, saying the boys were still lying three miles from Gregg Landing and had not had a fight yet ; that the rebels were waiting on them and they on the rebels, and each were holding their own ; also that General Sherman had taken Fort McAllister, eight miles from Savannah. After receiving this letter I wanted to get to Beaufort, so I could be near to them and so be able to get news from my husband. November

23 I got a pass for Beaufort. I arrived at Hilton Head about three o'clock next day, but there had been a battle, and a steamer arrived with a number of wounded men; so I could not get a transfer to Beaufort. The doctor wished me to remain over until Monday. I did not want to stay. I was anxious to get off, as I knew no one at Hilton Head.

I must mention a pet pig we had on Cole Island. Colonel Trowbridge brought into camp, one day, a poor, thin little pig, which a German soldier brought back with him on his return from a furlough. His regiment, the 74th Pennsylvania, was just embarking for the North, where it was ordered to join the 10th corps, and he could not take the pig back with him, so he gave it to our colonel. That pig grew to be the pet of the camp, and was the special care of the drummer boys, who taught him many tricks; and so well did they train him that every day at practice and dress parade, his pigship would march out with them, keeping perfect time with their music. The drummers would often disturb the devotions by riding this pig into the midst of evening praise meeting, and many were the complaints made to the colonel, but he was always very lenient towards the boys, for he knew they only did this for mischief. I shall never forget the fun we had in camp with " Piggie."

Portrait of the commander of
King's regiment, Col. Thomas
Wentworth Higginson.
From the original 1902 edition.

Portrait of four of Taylor's comrades with the
Thirty-third USCT (*clockwise from top*): Capt. L. W.
Metcalf, Capt. A. W. Jackson, Cpl. Peter Waggall, and
Capt. Miron W. Saxton. From the original 1902 edition.

Portrait of three of Taylor's comrades with the
Thirty-third USCT: Maj. H. A. Whitney (*top left*),
Lt. J. B. West (*top right*), and Henry Batchlott (*bottom*),
steward of the *John Adams*. From the original 1902 edition.

The bombardment of Fort Pulaski (*above*)
and the destruction of the fort.
Courtesy of the Georgia Historical Society.

Above, Christ Episcopal Church of Savannah.
Below, the Savannah docks after the Civil War.
Courtesy of the Georgia Historical Society.

A portrait of Lt. Col. Charles Trowbridge,
one of Taylor's favorite regimental officers.
From the original 1902 edition.

Portrait of Matilda Beasley,
Susie King Taylor's teacher in Savannah.
Courtesy of the Georgia Historical Society.

Taylor's schoolhouse in Savannah.
From the original 1902 edition.

VII

THERE was a yacht that carried passengers from Hilton Head to Beaufort. There were also five small boats which carried people over. The only people here, beside the soldiers, were Mrs. Lizzie Brown, who came over on a permit to see her husband, who was at this place, and was very ill (he died while she was there), Corporal Walker's wife, with her two years old child, and Mrs. Seabrooke. As soon as we could get the yacht, these persons I have mentioned, together with a comrade just discharged, an officer's boy, and myself, took passage on it for Beaufort. It was nearly dark before we had gone any distance, and about eight o'clock we were cast away and were only saved through the mercy of God. I remember going down twice. As I rose the second time, I caught hold of the sail and managed to hold fast. Mrs. Walker held on to her child with one hand, while with the other she managed to hold fast to some part of the boat, and we drifted and shouted as loud as we could, trying to attract the attention of some of the government boats which were going up and down the river. But it was in vain, we could not make ourselves heard, and just when we gave up all hope, and in the last moment (as we thought) gave one more despairing cry, we were heard at Ladies' Island. Two boats were put off and a search was made, to locate our distressed boat. They found us at last, nearly dead from exposure. In fact, the poor little baby was dead, although her mother still held her by her clothing, with her teeth. The soldier was drowned, having been caught under the sail and pinned down. The rest of us were saved. I had to be carried bodily, as I was thoroughly exhausted. We were given the best attention that we could get at this place where we were picked up. The men who saved us were surprised when they found me among the passengers, as one of them, William Geary, of Darien, Georgia, was a friend of my husband. His mother lived about two miles from where we were picked up, and she told me she had heard cries for a long time that night, and was very uneasy about it. Finally, she said to her son, " I think some poor souls are cast away." " I don't think so, mother," he replied ; " I saw some people going down the river to-day. You know this is Christmas, and they are having a good time." But she still persisted that these were cries of distress, and not of joy, and begged him to go out and see. So to satisfy her, he went outside and listened, and then he heard them also, and hastened to get the boats off to find us. We were capsized about 8.15 P. M. and it was near midnight when they found us. Next day, they kept a sharp lookout on the beach for anything that might be washed in from the yacht, and got a trunk and several other things. Had the tide been going out, we should have been carried to sea and lost.

I was very ill and under the doctor's care for some time, in Beaufort. The doctor said I ought to have been rolled, as I had swallowed so much water. In January, 1865, I went back to Cole Island, where I could be attended by my doctor, Dr. Miner, who did all in his power to alleviate my suffering, for I was swollen very much. This he reduced and I recovered, but had a severe cough for a long time afterward.

VIII

In October, 1864, six companies of the regiment were ordered to Gregg Landing, S. C. Captain L. W. Metcalf, of Co. G, was appointed on General Saxton's staff as provost captain, Lieutenant James B. West acting as assistant general. As in some way our mail had been sent over to the Confederate side and their mail to us, Captain Metcalf and Lieutenant West were detailed to exchange these letters under a flag of truce. So, with an escort of six men of the companies at Port Royal Ferry, the flag was unfurled and the message shouted across the river to the Confederates. Captain Metcalf asked them to come over to our side under the protection of our flag of truce. This the Confederates refused to do, having for their excuse that their boat was too far up the river and so they had no way to cross the river to us. They asked Metcalf to cross to them. He at once ordered his men to "stack arms," the Confederates following suit, and his boys in blue rowed him over, and he delivered the message, after having introduced himself to the rebel officers. One of these officers was Major Jones, of Alabama, the other Lieutenant Scott, of South Carolina. Major Jones was very cordial to our captain, but Lieutenant Scott would not extend his hand, and stood aside, in sullen silence, looking as if he would like to take revenge then and there. Major Jones said to Captain Metcalf, " We have no one to fight for. Should I meet you again, I shall not forget we have met before." With this he extended his hand to Metcalf and bade him good-by, but Lieutenant Scott stood by and looked as cross as he possibly could. The letters were exchanged, but it seemed a mystery just how those letters got missent to the opposite sides. Captain Metcalf said he did not feel a mite comfortable while he was on the Confederate soil ; as for his men, you can imagine their thoughts. I asked them how they felt on the other side, and they said, " We would have felt much better if we had had our guns with us." It was a little risky, for sometimes the flag of truce is not regarded, but even among the enemy there are some good and loyal persons.

Captain Metcalf is still living in Medford. He is 71 years old, and just as loyal to the old flag and the G. A. R. as he was from 1861 to 1866, when he was mustered out. He was a brave captain, a good officer, and was honored and beloved by all in the regiment.

IX

On February 28, 1865, the remainder of the
regiment were ordered to Charleston, as there
were signs of the rebels evacuating that city.
Leaving Cole Island, we arrived in Charleston
between nine and ten o'clock in the morning, and
found the " rebs " had set fire to the city and fled,
leaving women and children behind to suffer and
perish in the flames. The fire had been burning
fiercely for a day and night. When we landed,
under a flag of truce, our regiment went to work
assisting the citizens in subduing the flames. It
was a terrible scene. For three or four days the
men fought the fire, saving the property and
effects of the people, yet these white men and
women could not tolerate our black Union soldiers, for many of them had formerly been their
slaves ; and although these brave men risked life
and limb to assist them in their distress, men
and even women would sneer and molest them
whenever they met them.

I had quarters assigned me at a residence on
South Battery Street, one of the most aristocratic
parts of the city, where I assisted in caring for

the sick and injured comrades.   After getting the
fire under control, the regiment marched out to
the race track, where they camped until March
12, when we were ordered to Savannah, Ga.
We arrived there on the 13th, about eight o'clock
in the evening, and marched out to Fairlong, near
the A. & G. R. R., where we remained about ten
days, when we were ordered to Augusta, Ga.,
where Captain Alexander Heasley, of Co. E,
was shot and killed by a Confederate.   After his
death Lieutenant Parker was made captain of the
company, and was with us until the regiment was
mustered out.   He often told me about Massachusetts, but I had no thought at that time that
I should ever see that State, and stand in the
" Cradle of Liberty."

The regiment remained in Augusta for thirty
days, when it was ordered to Hamburg, S. C., and
then on to Charleston.   It was while on their
march through the country, to the latter city,
that they came in contact with the bushwhackers (as the rebels were called), who hid in the
bushes and would shoot the Union boys every
chance they got.   Other times they would conceal
themselves in the cars used to transfer our soldiers,
and when our boys, worn out and tired, would fall
asleep, these men would come out from their hiding places and cut their throats.   Several of our
men were killed in this way, but it could not be
found out who was committing these murders un-

til one night one of the rebels was caught in the
act, trying to cut the throat of a sleeping soldier.   He was put under guard, court-martialed,
and shot at Wall Hollow.

First Lieutenant Jerome T. Furman and a number of soldiers were killed by these South Carolina
bushwhackers at Wall Hollow.   After this man
was shot, however, the regiment marched through
unmolested to Charleston.

X

THE regiment, under Colonel Trowbridge, reached Charleston in November, 1865, and camped on the race track until January, when they returned to Morris Island, and on February 9, 1866, the following " General Orders " were received and the regiment mustered out.

They were delighted to go home, but oh ! how they hated to part from their commanding chief, Colonel C. T. Trowbridge. He was the very first officer to take charge of black soldiers. We thought there was no one like him, for he was a " man " among his soldiers. All in the regiment knew him personally, and many were the jokes he used to tell them. I shall never forget his friendship and kindness toward me, from the first time I met him to the end of the war. There was never any one from the North who came into our camp but he would bring them to see me.

While on a visit South in 1888, I met a comrade of the regiment, who often said to me, " You up North, Mrs. King, do you ever see Colonel Trowbridge ? How I should like to see him ! I don't see why he does not come South sometime.

Why, I would take a day off and look up all the
' boys ' I could find, if I knew he was coming."
I knew this man meant what he said, for the men
of the regiment knew Colonel Trowbridge first of
all the other officers.   He was with them on St.
Simon and at Camp Saxton.   I remember when
the company was being formed, we wished Captain C. T. was our captain, because most of the
men in Co. E were the men he brought with him
from St. Simon, and they were attached to him.
He was always jolly and pleasing with all.   I remember, when going into Savannah in 1865, he
said that he had been there before the war, and
told me many things I did not know about the
river.   Although this was my home, I had never
been on it before.   No officer in the army was
more beloved than our late lieutenant-colonel, C.
T. Trowbridge.

[Copy of General Orders.]

" GENERAL ORDERS.

" HEADQUARTERS 33D U. S. C. T.,
" LATE 1ST SO. CAROLINA VOLUNTEERS,
" MORRIS ISLAND, S. C., Feb. 9, 1866.

" *General Order,* ⎫
   " *No.* 1.   ⎬

" COMRADES : The hour is at hand when we
must separate forever, and nothing can take from
us the pride we feel, when we look upon the history of the ' First South Carolina Volunteers,'

the first black regiment that ever bore arms in defense of freedom on the continent of America.

" On the 9th day of May, 1862, at which time there were nearly four millions of your race in bondage, sanctioned by the laws of the land and protected by our flag, — on that day, in the face of the floods of prejudice that well-nigh deluged every avenue to manhood and true liberty, you came forth to do battle for your country and kindred.

" For long and weary months, without pay or even the privilege of being recognized as soldiers, you labored on, only to be disbanded and sent to your homes without even a hope of reward, and when our country, necessitated by the deadly struggle with armed traitors, finally granted you the opportunity again to come forth in defense of the nation's life, the alacrity with which you responded to the call gave abundant evidence of your readiness to strike a manly blow for the liberty of your race. And from that little band of hopeful, trusting, and brave men who gathered at Camp Saxton, on Port Royal Island, in the fall of '62, amidst the terrible prejudices that surrounded us, has grown an army of a hundred and forty thousand black soldiers, whose valor and heroism has won for your race a name which will live as long as the undying pages of history shall endure ; and by whose efforts, united with those of the white man, armed rebellion has been conquered, the millions of bondsmen have been emancipated, and the fundamental law of the land has been so altered as to remove forever the possibility of human slavery being established within the borders of redeemed America. The flag of our fathers, restored to its rightful significance, now floats over every foot of our territory, from Maine to California, and beholds only free men! The prejudices which formerly existed against you are well-nigh rooted out.

" Soldiers, you have done your duty and acquitted yourselves like men who, actuated by such ennobling motives, could not fail; and as the result of your fidelity and obedience you have won your freedom, and oh, how great the reward! It seems fitting to me that the last hours of our existence as a regiment should be passed amidst the unmarked graves of your comrades, at Fort Wagner. Near you rest the bones of Colonel Shaw, buried by an enemy's hand in the same grave with his black soldiers who fell at his side; where in the future your children's children will come on pilgrimages to do homage to the ashes of those who fell in this glorious struggle.

" The flag which was presented to us by the Rev. George B. Cheever and his congregation, of New York city, on the 1st of January, 1863, — the day when Lincoln's immortal proclamation of freedom was given to the world, — and which you have borne so nobly through the war, is now to be rolled up forever and deposited in our nation's capital. And while there it shall rest, with the battles in which you have participated inscribed upon its folds, it will be a source of pride to us all to remember that it has never been disgraced by a cowardly faltering in the hour of danger, or polluted by a traitor's touch.

"Now that you are to lay aside your arms, I adjure you, by the associations and history of the past, and the love you bear for your liberties, to harbor no feelings of hatred toward your former masters, but to seek in the paths of honesty, virtue, sobriety, and industry, and by a willing obedience to the laws of the land, to grow up to the full stature of American citizens. The church, the school-house, and the right forever to be free are now secured to you, and every prospect before you is full of hope and encouragement. The nation guarantees to you full protection and justice, and will require from you in return that respect for the laws and orderly deportment which will prove to every one your right to all the privileges of freemen. To the officers of the regiment I would say, your toils are ended, your mission is fulfilled, and we separate forever. The fidelity, patience, and patriotism with which you have discharged your duties to your men and to your country entitle you to a far higher tribute than any words of thankfulness which I can give you from the bottom of my heart. You will find your reward in the proud conviction that the cause for which you have battled so nobly has been crowned with abundant success.

" Officers and soldiers of the 33d U. S. Colored Troops, once the First So. Carolina Volunteers, I bid you all farewell!

" By order of

" Lt. Colonel C. T. Trowbridge,

" *Commanding regiment.*

" E. W. Hyde,

" 1st Lieut. 33d U. S. C. T. and acting adjutant."

I have one of the original copies of these orders still in my possession.

My dear friends! do we understand the meaning of war? Do we know or think of that war of '61? No, we do not, only those brave soldiers, and those who had occasion to be in it, can realize what it was. I can and shall never forget that terrible war until my eyes close in death. The scenes are just as fresh in my mind to-day as in '61. I see now each scene, — the roll-call, the drum tap, " lights out," the call at night when there was danger from the enemy, the double force of pickets, the cold and rain. How anxious I would be, not knowing what would happen before morning! Many times I would dress, not sure but all would be captured. Other times I would stand at my tent door and try to see what was going on, because night was the time the

rebels would try to get into our lines and capture
some of the boys. It was mostly at night that
our men went out for their scouts, and often had
a hand to hand fight with the rebels, and although
our men came out sometimes with a few killed
or wounded, none of them ever were captured.

We do not, as the black race, properly appreciate the old veterans, white or black, as we
ought to. I know what they went through, especially those black men, for the Confederates had
no mercy on them ; neither did they show any
toward the white Union soldiers. I have seen
the terrors of that war. I was the wife of one
of those men who did not get a penny for eighteen months for their services, only their rations
and clothing.

I cannot praise General David Hunter too
highly, for he was the first man to arm the black
man, in the beginning of 1862. He had a hard
struggle to hold all the southern division, with
so few men, so he applied to Congress ; but the
answer to him was, " Do not bother us," which
was very discouraging. As the general needed
more men to protect the islands and do garrison
duty, he organized two companies.

I look around now and see the comforts that
our younger generation enjoy, and think of the
blood that was shed to make these comforts possible for them, and see how little some of them
appreciate the old soldiers. My heart burns

within me, at this want of appreciation.   There
are only a few of them left now, so let us all, as
the ranks close, take a deeper interest in them.
Let the younger generation take an interest also,
and remember that it was through the efforts of
these veterans that they and we older ones enjoy
our liberty to-day.

XI

AFTER THE WAR

In 1866, the steamers which ran from Savannah to Darien would not take colored people unless they stayed in a certain part of the boat, away from the white people; so some of the colored citizens and ex-soldiers decided to form a syndicate and buy a steamer of their own. They finally bought a large one of a New York company. It arrived in fine shape, apparently, and made its first trip to Darien. The next trip was to Beaufort. I went on this trip, as the pilot, James Cook, was a friend of my family, and I thought I would enjoy the trip; and I did, getting back in safety. The next trip was to go to Florida, but it never reached there, for on the way down the boat ran upon St. John bar and went entirely to pieces. They found out afterwards that they had been swindled, as the boat was a condemned one, and the company took advantage of them; and as they carried no insurance on the boat they lost all the money they had invested in it. The best people of the city expressed great sympathy for them in their loss, as it promised to prove a great investment at first.

At the close of the war, my husband and I returned to Savannah, a number of the comrades returning at the same time. A new life was before us now, all the old life left behind. After getting settled, I opened a school at my home on South Broad Street, now called Oglethorpe Avenue, as there was not any public school for negro children. I had twenty children at my school, and received one dollar a month for each pupil. I also had a few older ones who came at night. There were several other private schools besides mine. Mrs. Lucinda Jackson had one on the same street I lived on.

I taught almost a year, when the Beach Institute opened, which took a number of my scholars, as this was a free school. On September 16, 1866, my husband, Sergeant King, died, leaving me soon to welcome a little stranger alone. He was a boss carpenter, but being just mustered out of the army, and the prejudice against his race being still too strong to insure him much work at his trade, he took contracts for unloading vessels, and hired a number of men to assist him. He was much respected by the citizens, and was a general favorite with his associates.

In December, 1866, I was obliged to give up teaching, but in April, 1867, I opened a school in Liberty County, Georgia, and taught there one year ; but country life did not agree with me, so I returned to the city, and Mrs. Susie Carrier took charge of my school.

On my return to Savannah, I found that the free school had taken all my former pupils, so I opened a night school, where I taught a number of adults. This, together with other things I could get to do and the assistance of my brother-in-law, supported me. I taught this school until the fall of 1868, when a free night school opened at the Beach Institute, and again my scholars left me to attend this free school. So I had to close my school. I put my baby with my mother and entered in the employ of a family, where I lived quite a while, but had to leave, as the work was too hard.

In 1872 I put in a claim for my husband's bounty and received one hundred dollars, some of which I put in the Freedmen's Savings Bank. In the fall of 1872 I went to work for a very wealthy lady, Mrs. Charles Green, as laundress. In the spring of 1873, Mr. and Mrs. Green came North to Rye Beach for the summer, and as their cook did not care to go so far from home, I went with them in her place. While there, I won a prize for excellent cooking at a fair which the ladies who were summering there had held to raise funds to build an Episcopal Church, and Mrs. Green was one of the energetic workers to make this fair a success; and it was a success in every respect and a tidy sum was netted.

I returned South with Mrs. Green, and soon after, she went to Europe. I returned to Boston

again in 1874, through the kindness of Mrs.
Barnard, a daughter of ex-Mayor Otis of Boston.
She was accompanied by her husband, Mr. James
Barnard (who was an agent for the line of
steamers), her six children, the nurse, and myself. We left Savannah on the steamship Semi-
nole, under Captain Matthews, and when we had
passed Hatteras some distance, she broke her
shaft. The captain had the sails hoisted and we
drifted along, there being a stiff breeze, which
was greatly in our favor. Captain Matthews said
the nearest point he could make was Cape Henry
Light. About noon, Mr. Barnard spied the light
and told the captain if he would give him a boat
and some of the crew, he would row to the light
for help. This was done, the boat was manned
and they put off. They made the light, then
they made for Norfolk, which was eight miles from
the light, and did not reach the city until eight
o'clock that night.

Next morning he returned with a tug, to tow
us into Norfolk for repairs ; but the tug was too
small to move the steamer, so it went back for
more help, but before it returned, a Norfolk
steamer, on its way to Boston, stopped to see what
was the matter with our steamer. Our trouble
was explained to them, and almost all the passengers were transferred to this steamer. Mr. Barnard remained on the steamer, and Mrs. Barnard
deciding to remain with him, I went aboard this

other steamer with the rest of the passengers. We left them at anchor, waiting for the tugs to return.

This accident brought back very vividly the time previous to this, when I was in that other wreck in 1864, and I wondered if they would reach port safe, for it is a terrible thing to be cast away; but on arriving in Boston, about two days later, I was delighted to hear of the arrival of their steamer at T Wharf, with all on board safe.

Soon after I got to Boston, I entered the service of Mr. Thomas Smith's family, on Walnut Avenue, Boston Highlands, where I remained until the death of Mrs. Smith. I next lived with Mrs. Gorham Gray, Beacon Street, where I remained until I was married, in 1879, to Russell L. Taylor.

In 1880 I had another experience in steamer accidents. Mr. Taylor and I started for New York on the steamer Stonington. We were in bed when, sometime in the night, the Narragansett collided with our boat. I was awakened by the crash. I was in the ladies' cabin. There were about thirty-five or forty others in the cabin. I sprang out of my berth, dressed as quickly as I could, and tried to reach the deck, but we found the cabin door locked, and two men stood outside and would not let us out. About twenty minutes after, they opened the doors and we went up on deck, and a terrible scene was before us. The

Narragansett was on fire, in a bright blaze; the water was lighted as far as one could see, the passengers shrieking, groaning, running about, leaping into the water, panic-stricken. A steamer came to our assistance; they put the life-rafts off and saved a great many from the burning steamer, and picked a number up from the water. A colored man saved his wife and child by giving each a chair and having them jump overboard. These chairs kept them afloat until they were taken aboard by the life-raft. The steamer was burned to the water's edge. The passengers on board our steamer were transferred to another one and got to New York at 9.30 the next morning. A number of lives were lost in this accident, and the bow of the Stonington was badly damaged. I was thankful for my escape, for I had been in two similar experiences and got off safely, and I have come to the conclusion I shall never have a watery grave.

XII

ALL this time my interest in the boys in blue
had not abated. I was still loyal and true,
whether they were black or white. My hands
have never left undone anything they could do
towards their aid and comfort in the twilight of
their lives. In 1886 I helped to organize Corps
67, Women's Relief Corps, auxiliary to the G. A.
R., and it is a very flourishing corps to-day. I
have been Guard, Secretary, Treasurer for three
years, and in 1893 I was made President of this
corps, Mrs. Emily Clark being Department President this year. In 1896, in response to an order
sent out by the Department W. R. C. to take a
census to secure a complete roster of the Union
Veterans of the war of the Rebellion now resid-
ing in Massachusetts, I was allotted the West
End district, which (with the assistance of Mrs.
Lizzie L. Johnson, a member of Corps 67, and
widow of a soldier of the 54th Mass. Volunteers)
I canvassed with splendid success, and found a
great many comrades who were not attached to
any post in the city or State.

In 1898 the Department of Mass. W. R. C.

gave a grand fair at Music Hall. I made a large
quilt of red, white, and blue ribbon that made
quite a sensation. The quilt was voted for and
was awarded to the Department President, Mrs.
E. L. W. Waterman, of Boston.

XIII

THOUGHTS ON PRESENT CONDITIONS

LIVING here in Boston where the black man is given equal justice, I must say a word on the general treatment of my race, both in the North and South, in this twentieth century. I wonder if our white fellow men realize the true sense or meaning of brotherhood? For two hundred years we had toiled for them; the war of 1861 came and was ended, and we thought our race was forever freed from bondage, and that the two races could live in unity with each other, but when we read almost every day of what is being done to my race by some whites in the South, I sometimes ask, "Was the war in vain? Has it brought freedom, in the full sense of the word, or has it not made our condition more hopeless?"

In this "land of the free" we are burned, tortured, and denied a fair trial, murdered for any imaginary wrong conceived in the brain of the negro-hating white man. There is no redress for us from a government which promised to protect all under its flag. It seems a mystery to me. They say, "One flag, one nation, one country indivisible." Is this true? Can we say this truthfully, when one race is allowed to burn, hang, and inflict the most horrible torture weekly, monthly, on another? No, we cannot sing, "My country, 't is of thee, Sweet land of Liberty"! It is hollow mockery. The Southland laws are all on the side of the white, and they do just as they like to the negro, whether in the right or not.

I do not uphold my race when they do wrong. They ought to be punished, but the innocent are made to suffer as well as the guilty, and I hope the time will hasten when it will be stopped forever. Let us remember God says, "He that sheds blood, his blood shall be required again." I may not live to see it, but the time is approaching when the South will again have cause to repent for the blood it has shed of innocent black men, for their blood cries out for vengeance. For the South still cherishes a hatred toward the blacks, although there are some true Southern gentlemen left who abhor the stigma brought upon them, and feel it very keenly, and I hope the day is not far distant when the two races will reside in peace in the Southland, and we will sing with sincere and truthful hearts, "My country, 't is of thee, Sweet land of Liberty, of thee I sing."

I have been in many States and cities, and in each I have looked for liberty and justice, equal for the black as for the white ; but it was not until I was within the borders of New England, and reached old Massachusetts, that I found it.

Here is found liberty in the full sense of the word, liberty for the stranger within her gates, irrespective of race or creed, liberty and justice for all.

We have before us still another problem to solve. With the close of the Spanish war, and on the entrance of the Americans into Cuba, the same conditions confront us as the war of 1861 left. The Cubans are free, but it is a limited freedom, for prejudice, deep-rooted, has been brought to them and a separation made between the white and black Cubans, a thing that had never existed between them before ; but to-day there is the same intense hatred toward the negro in Cuba that there is in some parts of this country.

I helped to furnish and pack boxes to be sent to the soldiers and hospitals during the first part of the Spanish war; there were black soldiers there too. At the battle of San Juan Hill, they were in the front, just as brave, loyal, and true as those other black men who fought for freedom and the right; and yet their bravery and faithfulness were reluctantly acknowledged, and praise grudgingly given. All we ask for is " equal justice," the same that is accorded to all other races who come to this country, of their free will (not forced to, as we were), and are allowed to enjoy every privilege, unrestricted, while we are denied what is rightfully our own

in a country which the labor of our forefathers
helped to make what it is.

One thing I have noticed among my people in
the South : they have accumulated a large amount
of real estate, far surpassing the colored owners
in the North, who seem to let their opportunity
slip by them. Nearly all of Brownsville (a sub-
urb of Savannah) is owned by colored people,
and so it is in a great many other places throughout the State, and all that is needed is the protection of the law as citizens.

In 1867, soon after the death of my father,
who had served on a gunboat during the war,
my mother opened a grocery store, where she
kept general merchandise always on hand. These
she traded for cash or would exchange for crops
of cotton, corn, or rice, which she would ship once
a month, to F. Lloyd & Co., or Johnson &
Jackson, in Savannah. These were colored mer-
chants, doing business on Bay Street in that city.
Mother bought her first property, which contained
ten acres. She next purchased fifty acres of land.
Then she had a chance to get a place with seven
hundred acres of land, and she bought this.

In 1870, Colonel Hamilton and Major Devendorft, of Oswego, N. Y., came to the town and
bought up a tract of land at a place called Doctortown, and started a mill. Mrs. Devendorft
heard of my mother and went to see her, and persuaded her to come to live with her, assuring her

she would be as one of the family. Mother went
with her, but after a few months she went to
Doctortown, where she has been since, and now
owns the largest settlement there. All trains
going to Florida pass her place, just across the
Altamaha River. She is well known by both
white and black; the people are fond of her, and
will not allow any one to harm her.

Mr. Devendorft sold out his place in 1880 and
went back to New York, where later he died.

I read an article, which said the ex-Confeder-
ate Daughters had sent a petition to the mana-
gers of the local theatres in Tennessee to prohibit
the performance of " Uncle Tom's Cabin," claim-
ing it was exaggerated (that is, the treatment of
the slaves), and would have a very bad effect on
the children who might see the drama. I paused
and thought back a few years of the heart-rend-
ing scenes I have witnessed; I have seen many
times, when I was a mere girl, thirty or forty
men, handcuffed, and as many women and children, come every first Tuesday of each month
from Mr. Wiley's trade office to the auction
blocks, one of them being situated on Drayton
Street and Court Lane, the other on Bryant
Street, near the Pulaski House. The route was
down our principal street, Bull Street, to the
court-house, which was only a block from where
I resided.

All people in those days got all their water

from the city pumps, which stood about a block apart throughout the city. The one we used to get water from was opposite the court-house, on Bull Street. I remember, as if it were yesterday, seeing droves of negroes going to be sold, and I often went to look at them, and I could hear the auctioneer very plainly from my house, auctioning these poor people off.

Do these Confederate Daughters ever send petitions to prohibit the atrocious lynchings and wholesale murdering and torture of the negro? Do you ever hear of them fearing this would have a bad effect on the children? Which of these two, the drama or the present state of affairs, makes a degrading impression upon the minds of our young generation? In my opinion it is not "Uncle Tom's Cabin," but it should be the one that has caused the world to cry "Shame!" It does not seem as if our land is yet civilized. It is like times long past, when rulers and high officers had to flee for their lives, and the negro has been dealt with in the same way since the war by those he lived with and toiled for two hundred years or more. I do not condemn all the Caucasian race because the negro is badly treated by a few of the race. No! for had it not been for the true whites, assisted by God and the prayers of our forefathers, I should not be here to-day.

There are still good friends to the negro.

Why, there are still thousands that have not bowed to Baal. So it is with us. Man thinks two hundred years is a long time, and it is, too; but it is only as a week to God, and in his own time — I know I shall not live to see the day, but it will come — the South will be like the North, and when it comes it will be prized higher than we prize the North to-day. God is just; when he created man he made him in his image, and never intended one should misuse the other. All men are born free and equal in his sight.

I am pleased to know at this writing that the officers and comrades of my regiment stand ready to render me assistance whenever required. It seems like "bread cast upon the water," and it has returned after many days, when it is most needed. I have received letters from some of the comrades, since we parted in 1866, with expressions of gratitude and thanks to me for teaching them their first letters. One of them, Peter Waggall, is a minister in Jacksonville, Fla. Another is in the government service at Washington, D. C. Others are in Darien and Savannah, Ga., and all are doing well.

There are many people who do not know what some of the colored women did during the war. There were hundreds of them who assisted the Union soldiers by hiding them and helping them to escape. Many were punished for taking food to the prison stockades for the prisoners. When I

went into Savannah, in 1865, I was told of one of
these stockades which was in the suburbs of the
city, and they said it was an awful place.   The
Union soldiers were in it, worse than pigs, without
any shelter from sun or storm, and the colored
women would take food there at night and pass it
to them, through the holes in the fence. The soldiers were starving, and these women did all they
could towards relieving those men, although they
knew the penalty, should they be caught giving
them aid.   Others assisted in various ways the
Union army.   These things should be kept in
history before the people.   There has never been
a greater war in the United States than the one
of 1861, where so many lives were lost, — not men
alone but noble women as well.

Let us not forget that terrible war, or our
brave soldiers who were thrown into Anderson-
ville and Libby prisons, the awful agony they
went through, and the most brutal treatment they
received in those loathsome dens, the worst ever
given human beings ; and if the white soldiers
were subjected to such treatment, what must have
been the horrors inflicted on the negro soldiers
in their prison pens ?   Can we forget those cruel-
ties ?   No, though we try to forgive and say,
" No North, no South," and hope to see it in reality before the last comrade passes away.

XIV

THE inevitable always happens. On February 3, 1898, I was called to Shreveport, La., to the bedside of my son, who was very ill. He was traveling with Nickens and Company, with "The Lion's Bride," when he fell ill, and had been ill two weeks when they sent to me. I tried to have him brought home to Boston, but they could not send him, as he was not able to sit and ride this long distance; so on the sixth of February I left Boston to go to him. I reached Cincinnati on the eighth, where I took the train for the south. I asked a white man standing near (before I got my train) what car I should take. "Take that one," he said, pointing to one. "But that is a smoking car!" "Well," he replied, "that is the car for colored people." I went to this car, and on entering it all my courage failed me. I have ridden in many coaches, but I was never in such as these. I wanted to return home again, but when I thought of my sick boy I said, "Well, others ride in these cars and I must do likewise," and tried to be resigned, for I wanted to reach my boy, as I did not know whether I should find

him alive. I arrived in Chattanooga at eight
o'clock in the evening, where the porter took my
baggage to the train which was to leave for
Marion, Miss. Soon after I was seated, just
before the train pulled out, two tall men with
slouch hats on walked through the car, and on
through the train. Finally they came back to
our car and stopping at my seat said, "Where
are those men who were with you?" I did not
know to whom they were speaking, as there was
another woman in the car, so I made no reply.
Again they asked me, standing directly in front
of my seat, "Where are those men who came
in with you?" "Are you speaking to me?" I
said. "Yes!" they said. "I have not seen any
men," I replied. They looked at me a moment,
and one of them asked where I was from. I
told him Boston; he hesitated a minute and
walked out of our car to the other car.

When the conductor came around I told him
what these men had said, and asked him if they
allowed persons to enter the car and insult passengers. He only smiled. Later, when the porter
came in, I mentioned it to him. He said, "Lady,
I see you do not belong here; where are you
from?" I told him. He said, "I have often heard
of Massachusetts. I want to see that place."
"Yes!" I said, "you can ride there on the cars,
and no person would be allowed to speak to you
as those men did to me." He explained that those

men were constables, who were in search of a
man who had eloped with another man's wife.
" That is the way they do here.   Each morning
you can hear of some negro being lynched ; " and
on seeing my surprise, he said, " Oh, that is nothing ; it is done all the time.   We have no rights
here.   I have been on this road for fifteen years
and have seen some terrible things."   He wanted
to know what I was doing down there, and I told
him it was only the illness of my son that brought
me there.

I was a little surprised at the way the poor
whites were made to ride on this road.   They put
them all together by themselves in a car, between
the colored people's coach and the first-class coach,
and it looked like the " laborers' car " used in
Boston to carry the different day laborers to and
from their work.

I got to Marion, Miss., at two o'clock in the
morning, arrived at Vicksburg at noon, and at
Shreveport about eight o'clock in the evening,
and found my son just recovering from a severe
hemorrhage.   He was very anxious to come home,
and I tried to secure a berth for him on a sleeper,
but they would not sell me one, and he was not
strong enough to travel otherwise.   If I could only
have gotten him to Cincinnati, I might have
brought him home, but as I could not I was forced
to let him remain where he was.   It seemed very
hard, when his father fought to protect the Union

and our flag, and yet his boy was denied, under this same flag, a berth to carry him home to die, because he was a negro.

Shreveport is a little town, made up largely of Jews and Germans and a few Southerners, the negroes being in the majority. Its sidewalks are sand except on the main street. Almost all the stores are kept either by the Jews or Germans. They know a stranger in a minute, as the town is small and the citizens know each other; if not personally, their faces are familiar.

I went into a jewelry store one day to have a crystal put in my watch, and the attendant remarked, "You are a stranger." I asked him how he knew that. He said he had watched me for a week or so. I told him yes, I was a stranger and from Boston. "Oh! I have heard of Boston," he said. "You will not find this place like it is there. How do you like this town?" "Not very well," I replied.

I found that the people who had lived in Massachusetts and were settled in Shreveport were very cordial to me and glad to see me. There was a man murdered in cold blood for nothing. He was a colored man and a " porter " in a store in this town. A clerk had left his umbrella at home. It had begun to rain when he started for home, and on looking for the umbrella he could not, of course, find it. He asked the porter if he had seen it. He said no, he had not. " You

answer very saucy," said the clerk, and drawing
his revolver, he shot the colored man dead.   He
was taken up the street to an office where he was
placed under onè thousand dollars bond for his
appearance and released, and that was the end of
the case.   I was surprised at this, but I was told
by several white and colored persons that this was
a common occurrence, and the persons were never
punished if they were white, but no mercy was
shown to negroes.

I met several comrades, white and colored, there,
and noticed that the colored comrades did not
wear their buttons.   I asked one of them why this
was, and was told, should they wear it, they could
not get work.   Still some would wear their buttons in spite of the feeling against it.   I met a
newsman from New York on the train.   He was
a veteran, and said that Sherman ought to come
back and go into that part of the country.

Shreveport is a horrid place when it rains.
The earth is red and sticks to your shoes, and it
is impossible to keep rubbers on, for the mud pulls
them off.   Going across the Mississippi River, I
was amazed to see how the houses were built, so
close to the shore, or else on low land; and when
the river rises, it flows into these houses and must
make it very disagreeable and unhealthy for the
inmates.

After the death of my son, while on my way
back to Boston, I came to Clarksdale, one of the

stations on the road from Vicksburg. In this town a Mr. Hancock, of New York, had a large cotton plantation, and the Chinese intermarry with the blacks.

At Clarksdale, I saw a man hanged. It was a terrible sight, and I felt alarmed for my own safety down there. When I reached Memphis I found conditions of travel much better. The people were mostly Western and Northern here; the cars were nice, but separate for colored persons until we reached the Ohio River, when the door was opened and the porter passed through, saying, "The Ohio River! change to the other car." I thought, "What does he mean? We have been riding all this distance in separate cars, and now we are all to sit together." It certainly seemed a peculiar arrangement. Why not let the negroes, if their appearance and respectability warrant it, be allowed to ride as they do in the North, East, or West?

There are others beside the blacks, in the South and North, that should be put in separate cars while traveling, just as they put my race. Many black people in the South do not wish to be thrown into a car because all are colored, as there are many of their race very objectionable to them, being of an entirely different class; but they have to adapt themselves to the circumstances and ride with them, because they are all negroes. There is no such division with the whites. Except

in one place I saw, the workingman and the mil-
lionaire ride in the same coaches together. Why
not allow the respectable, law-abiding classes of
the blacks the same privilege? We hope for
better conditions in the future, and feel sure
they will come in time, surely if slowly.

While in Shreveport, I visited ex-Senator
Harper's house. He is a colored man and owns
a large business block, besides a fine residence
on Cado Street and several good building lots.
Another family, the Pages, living on the same
street, were quite wealthy, and a large number
of colored families owned their homes, and were
industrious, refined people; and if they were only
allowed justice, the South would be the only place
for our people to live.

We are similar to the children of Israel, who,
after many weary years in bondage, were led
into that land of promise, there to thrive and
be forever free from persecution; and I don't
despair, for the Book which is our guide through
life declares, " Ethiopia shall stretch forth her
hand."

What a wonderful revolution! In 1861 the
Southern papers were full of advertisements for
"slaves," but now, despite all the hindrances
and "race problems," my people are striving to
attain the full standard of all other races born
free in the sight of God, and in a number of in-
stances have succeeded. Justice we ask, — to be

citizens of these United States, where so many of our people have shed their blood with their white comrades, that the stars and stripes should never be polluted.

APPENDIX

ROSTER OF SURVIVORS OF THIRTY-THIRD UNITED STATES COLORED TROOPS

THE following are the names of officers and men as near as I have been able to reach.

Colonel T. W. Higginson.
Lieut.-Col. C. T. Trowbridge.

COMPANY A.

Capt. Charles E. Parker,
Lieut. John A. Trowbridge,
Lieut. J. B. West,
O.-Sergt. Joseph Holden,
1st Sergt. —— Hattent,
2d Sergt. Wm. Jackson,
Thomas Smith,
George Green,
Manly Gater,
Paul Jones,
Sancho Jenkins,
London Bailey,
Edmund Mack,
Andrew Perry,
Morris Williams,
James Dorsen,
Abel Haywood.

COMPANY B.

Capt. Wm. James,

O.-Sergt. Bob Bowling,
2d Sergt. Nathan Hagans,
3d Sergt. Cato Wright,
4th Sergt. Frederick Parker,
5th Sergt. Wm. Simmons,
Corp. Monday Stewart,
Corp. Allick Seymore,
Corp. Lazarus Fields,
Corp. Boson Green,
Corp. Steven Wright,
Corp. Carolina Hagans,
Corp. Richard Robinson,
David Hall,
Edward Houston,
Smart Givins,
John Mills,
Jacob Riley,
Frederick Procter,
Benj. Gordon,
Benj. Mason,
Sabe Natteal,

APPENDIX

Joseph Noyels,
Benj. Mackwell,
Thos. Hernandes,
Israel Choen,
Steplight Gordon,
Chas. Talbert,
Isaac Jenkins,
Morris Polite,
Robert Freeman,
Jacob Watson,
Benj. Managualt,
Richard Adams,
Mingo Singleton,
Toney Chapman,
Jos. Knowell,
Benj. Gardner.

COMPANY C.

Capt. A. W. Jackson,
2d Sergt. Billy Milton,
Corp. Peter Waggall,
Corp. Henry Abrams,
Martin Dickson, Drummer,
Roddrick Langs, Fifer,
Joseph Smith,
Solomon Major,
John Brown,
Bram Strowbridge,
Robert Trewell,
Jerry Fields,
Paul Fields,
William Johnson,
Bram Stoved,
Robert Mack,
Samuel Mack,
Jack Mack,

Simon Gatson,
Bob Bolden,
James Long,
O.-S. Frederick Brown.

COMPANY D.

Sergt. Isaiah Brown,
Luke Wright,
Dick Haywood,
Stephen Murrel,
Jos. Halsley,
Nathan Hazeby,
O.-Sergt. Robert Godwen,
Peter Johnson,
Cæsar Johnson,
Sampson Cuthbert.

COMPANY E.

Capt. N. G. Parker,
Corp. Jack Sallens,
Quaker Green,
Abram Fuller,
Levan Watkins,
Peter Chisholm,
Scipio Haywood,
Paul King,
Richard Howard,
Esau Kellison,
Chas. Armstrong,
Washington Demry,
Benj. King,
Luke Harris,
William Cummings.

COMPANY F.

Capt. John Thompson,
Sergt. Robert Vandross,

APPENDIX

Sergt. Cæsar Alston,
2d Sergt. Moses Green,
Corp. Samuel Mack,
Edmund Washington,
Isaac Jenkins,
Chas. Seymore,
Frank Grayson,
Bristow Eddy,
Abram Fields,
Joseph Richardson,
James Brown,
Frederick Tripp,
Frost Coleman,
Paul Coleman,
Robert Edward,
Milton Edward.

COMPANY G.
Capt. L. W. Metcalf,
Sergt. T. W. Long,
Corp. Prince Logan,
Corp. Mark Clark,
Corp. James Ash,
Corp. Henry Hamilton,
Roddrick Long,
Benjamin Turner,
David Wanton,
Benjamin Martin,
John Ryals,
Charles Williams,
Hogarth Williams,
Benjamin Wright,
Henry Harker.

COMPANY H.
Capt. W. W. Sampson,
1st Sergt. Jacob Jones,

2d Sergt. Thomas Fields,
Corp. A. Brown,
Corp. Emmanuel Washington,
Jackson Danner,
Joseph Wright,
Phillips Brown,
Luke Harris,
Lazarus Aikens,
Jonah Aikens,
Jacob Jones,
Thomas Howard,
William Williams,
Jack Parker,
Jack Ladson,
Poll McKee,
Lucius Baker.

COMPANY I.
2d Sergt. Daniel Spaulding,
Corp. Uandickpe,
Corp. Floward,
Corp. Thompson.

COMPANY K.
O.-Sergt. Harry Williams,
2d Sergt. Billy Coleman,
3d Sergt. Cæsar Oston,
Jacob Lance,
Jack Burns,
Wm. McLean,
Geo. Washington,
David Wright,
Jerry Mitchell,
Jackson Green,
David Putnam,

B. Lance,	Leon Simmons,
Ward McKen,	Prince White,
Edmond Cloud,	Stephen Jenkins.
Chance Mitchel,	

Quarter-Master Harry West.
Quarter-Master's Sergt., Edward Colvin.

A LIST OF THE BATTLES FOUGHT BY THE THIRTY-THIRD U. S. COLORED TROOPS, FORMERLY FIRST S. C. VOLUNTEERS.

Darien, Ga., and Ridge	1862
St. Mary's River and Hundred Pines . .	1862
Pocotaligo Bridge [1]	1862
Jacksonville, Fla.	1863
Township	1863
Mill Town Bluff [2]	1863
Hall Island	1863
Johns Island	1863
Coosaw River	1863
Combahee and Edisto [3]	1863
James Island [4]	1864
Honey Hill	1864

[1] Many prisoners and stores captured.

[2] Four prisoners captured.

[3] 300 prisoners captured.

[4] Fort Gregg captured.